BUSINESS LAW PART 1: THE INDIAN CONTRACT ACT, 1872

A SIMPLIFIED VERSION OF THE INDIAN CONTRACT ACT, 1872

M VASANTHA

Made with ♥ on the Notion Press Platform
www.notionpress.com

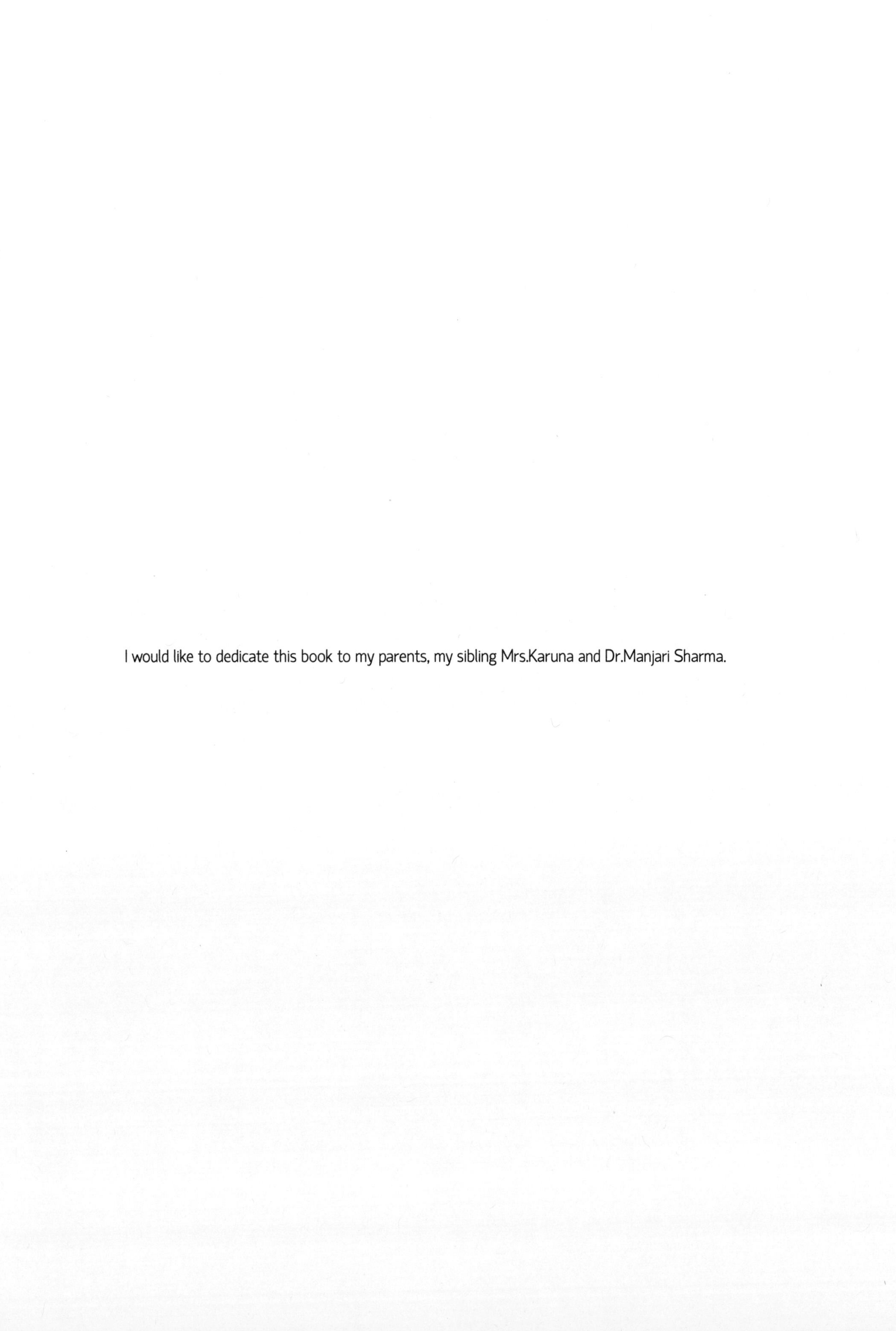

I would like to dedicate this book to my parents, my sibling Mrs.Karuna and Dr.Manjari Sharma.

Contents

Preface

As a student with no law base studying business law as a subject at the university was hard, even the text books availabe were also hard to understand and they had very few illustrtations, but then trying to link the law concepts to things around me made it easier to remeber and undersatnd the concepts better.

The main reason for me to write this, is to help the students studying business law understand the concepts in a better manner using illustrations and examples that they can relate to, relatability of the concepts is extremely important for students to understand and retain the concepts that they study.

Acknowledgements

Firstly, I would like to thank my parents, my sibling Mrs.Karuna & Secondly, my friends who have supported me all through the process of writing this book. Lastly, I would also like to thank Dr. Manjari Sharma for encouraging me to write and publish my work.

specially i would like to thank Mr.Srininvasa Abhai fro helping me edit and compile this book, and Ms.Garapatai Gowri Sathvika Chowdary and Mr.Anirudh Devarakonda fro constantly reading and giving a feedback to my work, without their constatnt support this book wouldnt have seen light of the day .

CHAPTER ONE

INTRODUCTION TO BUSINESS LAW

What is law?

A "set of regulations" as law aids in regulating behavior and creating a civilized society. Any authority, including a government or an organization, has the power to make laws.

Law has no set definition, as different jurists have different perceptions to law, but there are 5 theories of law:

1. Austin's command theory of law: John Austin is a legal thinker who held the university of London's first jurisprudence chair. The command theory of law is a trademark of Austin. Austin asserted that the law is the sovereign's command backed by sanctions, and he spread the idea that the law is a command that imposes obligations, the breach of which is punished with consequences (punishment) There are three key aspects of the command theory of law: It is a command that is supported by a sanction and is issued by a sovereign authority.
2. Roscoe Ponds Theory of Law: Renowned American legal scholar Roscoe Ponds was a prominent jurist of the 20th century and one of the most ardent supporters of Sociological Jurisprudence, placing special emphasis on the consideration of social facts in the formulation, interpretation, and application of law In his idea, Roscoe Pound found parallels between the work of an engineer and a lawyer. The objective of social theory was to create a social structure that satisfied the greatest number of desires with the least amount of friction and waste.
3. John William Salmond: John William Salmond taught law in New Zealand before becoming a judge on the country's highest court. In this way, Salmond was different from Bentham and Austin who focused on the analysis of the law as it was without considering its ultimate goal. Salmond argued that the goal of the law was to give justice to the people. Between "a law" and "the law," Salmond made a distinction, claiming that the former pertains to the concrete and the latter to the abstract.
4. Kelsen's "pure theory of law: Hans Kelsen was Austrian philosopher and a jurist who is a Known for his "pure theory of law". Kelsen described law as a "normative science distinguished from natural sciences which are based on cause & effect such as law of gravitation According to Kelson, `norm (sanctim) is rules forbidding prescribing Certain behaviour. d. According to Kelsen, we attach legal - - normative meaning to Certain actions and not to others depending on whether that event - Is accorded any legal normative by any other legal norm.
5. Bentham's theory of law: Jeremy Bentham was the pioneer Bentham said that every law. of analytical jurisprudence in Britain." be considered in 8 differentrespects.
   1 Source
   2 subjects
   3 objects
   4 Extent
   5 Aspects
   6 force
   7 Remedial appendage
   8 Expression
   ("JURISPRUDENCE, INTERPRETATION and GENERAL LAWS")

Evolution of Law

The concept of law encompasses fundamental moral guidelines as well as structures and tools for modifying, elaborating, clarifying, and enforcing the laws. Law is a natural result of people coexisting and cooperating. There must be a means of resolving the inevitable conflicts if people are to coexist. Applying rules to guide people's behavior can be viewed as the legal practice.

Before history was written, laws were gradually added as disagreements were resolved. This is how the evolution of law got its start. In actuality, society's formation of norms precedes the creation of both courts and written law. For thousands of years, only private & customary legal systems regulated human affairs. (Younkins)

Why did the Laws Evolve?

Numerous factors have contributed to the evolution and changes in law over the years. Among the primary causes are:

Literacy: As the nation's literacy rate rises, more people are beginning to understand their obligations and rights. As a result, they have begun to call for stricter laws and regulations to protect their interests. The Transgender Persons (Protection of Rights) Act, 2019, which was passed to improve the lives of transgender people in India, is an example of such legislation.

Entry of Britishers into the Country: Britishers who arrived in India discovered that the nation lacked a unified legal system, which made it simple for them to develop their empire there. Later, however, they understood that they needed a single law for everyone in the nation, regardless of their gender or religion, in order to maintain their reign, there. Thus, they established national law (common law).

Gender equality: The equality of men and women in all spheres of life is a concept that has grown significantly in relevance over time. A number of laws have been implemented to promote equality for all people, regardless of gender. According to Article 14 of the Indian Constitution, "The State shall not deny to any individual within the territory of India, equality before the law or the equal protection of the laws."

Progress in society: As society develops over time, some behaviours become highly prevalent, and as a result, the behaviour no longer qualifies as an offence. If such an act continues to be illegal, everyone who committed it must be held accountable. Since it is impossible to punish everyone in society, such an act is replaced by another. (garg)

Law is a subject that is constantly changing, including several revisions, and bringing about numerous improvements that can support and safeguard the beliefs of individuals. As time goes on, outdated laws will be replaced by new ones that act in accordance with both society and constitutional ideals.

Being a dynamic sphere, law will keep evolving and will continue to change and adapt itself to the Indian subcontinent as a whole.

Why is it important to understand the law?

Knowing the law is essential because breaking the law cannot be justified by ignorance in other words "ignorance of the law is not an excuse".

"There is no telling to what extent the excuse of ignorance might not be carried, it would be argued in nearly every case," stated Lord Ellenborough. Thus, the discussion above clarifies the meaning of the Latin proverb "Ignorantia legis neminem excusat," which says that a person's ignorance of the law shall not be an excuse. (chettoor)

Law, in general, is divided into several parts

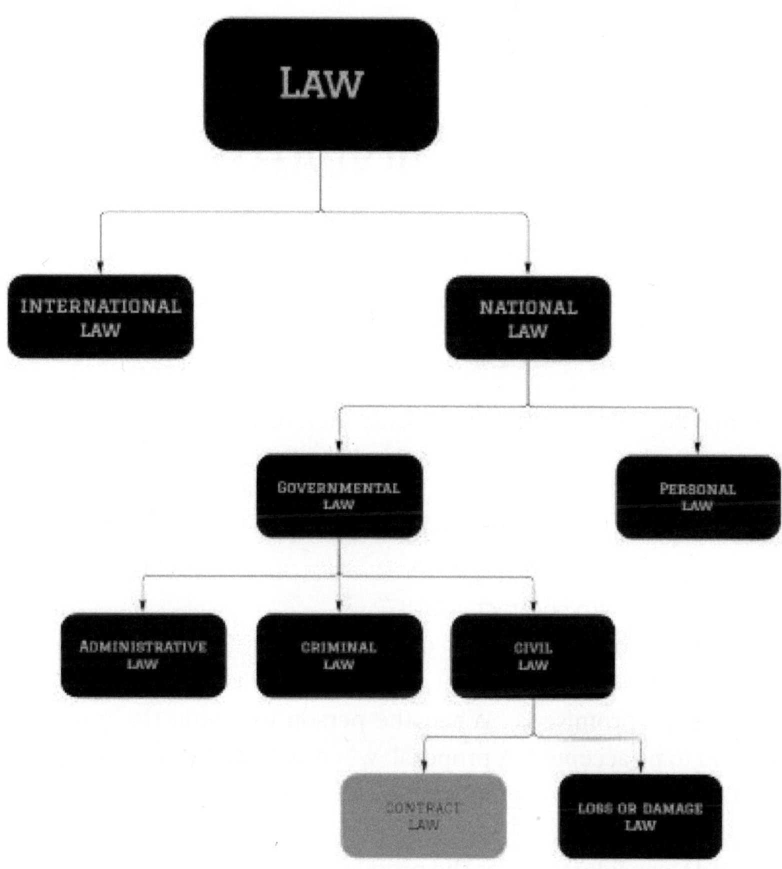

The whole set of business laws is known as "*Mercantile law*"

In this part, we mainly focus on Contract law (Indian Contract Act, 1872).

Why is it important to understand contract law in general?

Every person, whether knowingly or unknowingly, enters into several contracts every day; the contract law impacts everyone, but is most prominent in trade and business.

The Indian Contract Act of 1872 governs the law pertaining to contracts. The law came into effect on September 1st, 1872. The act is broken up into two sections: Section 1-75 deals with general contract principles and is thus relevant to all contracts regardless of their nature, and Section 124-238 deals with special types of contracts such as bailments and indemnification and guarantee.

The laws governing contracts are codified in the Indian Contract Act of 1872. The Act deals with certain types of commercial agreements, such as indemnification, guarantee, bailment, pledge, quasi-contracts, contingent contracts, etc., in addition to identifying the elements of a legally enforceable valid contract. It essentially lays out the conditions under which promises made by contracting parties shall be held to be legally enforceable.

This area of law differs significantly from other areas of law in a crucial way. It incorporates some limiting principles, subject to which the parties may construct rights and duties for themselves, rather than prescribing a high proportion of rights and obligations that the law will protect or enforce.

Now that you have understood the basics of law, let's just dive into the contract law.

CHAPTER TWO

INTRODUCTION TO INDIAN CONTRACT ACT

The Indian Contract Act, of 1872

Short title - This Act may be called the Indian Contract Act, of 1872.

Extent & commencement - the act applies to the whole of India including Jammu and Kashmir and it came into effect on 1st September 1872.

**Interpretation clause: expressly explains the parties' intent for specific grammatical rules to be construed in the contract. **

Interpretation clause for the Indian contract act 1872

According to section 2(a), a proposal is "When one person signifies to another his willingness to do or to abstain from doing anything, to obtain the assent of that other to such act or abstinence, he is said to propose"

According to section 2(b), a promise is "When the person to whom the proposal is made signifies his assent thereto, the proposal is said to be accepted. A proposal, when accepted, becomes a promise"

According to section 2(c), "The person proposing is called the 'promisor', and the person accepting the proposal is called the 'promisee'"

According to section 2(d), consideration for the promise is "When, at the desire of the promisor, the promisee or any other person has done or abstained from doing, or does or abstains from doing, or promises to do or to abstain from doing, something, such act or abstinence or promise"

According to section 2(e), "Every promise and every set of promises, forming the consideration for each other, is an agreement"

According to section 2(f), "Promises which form the consideration or part of the consideration for each other are called reciprocal promises"

According to section 2(g), a void agreement is "An agreement not enforceable by law is said to be void"

According to section 2(h), "An agreement enforceable by law is a contract"

According to section 2(i), "An agreement which is enforceable by law at the option of one or more of the parties thereto, but not at the option of the other or others, is a voidable contract"

According to section 2(j), "A contract which ceases to be enforceable by law becomes void when it ceases to be enforceable"

(*ARRANGEMENT of SECTIONS ____________ SECTIONS PREAMBLE*)

CHAPTER THREE

ELEMENTS, ESSENTIALS, AND TYPES OF CONTRACTS

Contracts are defined as “an agreement enforceable by law” in section 2(h) of the Indian contract act, of 1872.

Any contract consists of the following two essential elements:

1. An agreement
2. Enforceability by law

- The **agreement** is defined in section 2(e) of the Indian contract act 1872 as “Every promise and every set of promises, forming the consideration for each other, is an agreement”
  A promise according to section 2(b) is “When the person to whom the proposal is made signifies his assent thereto, the proposal is said to be accepted. A proposal, when accepted, becomes a promise”.
- **Enforceability** by law means an intention to create a legal obligation.

Agreement = Offer/proposal + Acceptance

Contract = accepted proposal/agreement + Enforceability by law

Example 1: Abhai promises his friend Barre that he will give 1 crore to Barre if he doesn’t get 100 marks in LAW, and Abhai go 99 marks but did not pay the 1 crore ?. Barre cannot recover this amount in a court of law as this was a social agreement. This did not have the intention to create a legal relationship and hence it is not a contract.

Example 2: Anirudh agrees with Satvika to sell his Law notebook for 500 ?. In this case, Anirudh is obligated to give satvika his law notebook and satvika is under an obligation to pay Anirudh 500 ? hence Anirudh has a right to receive 500 ? for the same.

<u>The basic difference between an agreement and a contract</u>:

Agreement	Contract
Every promise or every set of promises forms the consideration for each other.	An agreement that is enforceable by law.
Agreements are not enforceable in a court of law.	Contracts are enforceable in a court of law.
Agreements may or may not create a legal obligation. i.e., agreements can be both legal and social.	Contracts necessarily need to create a legal obligation.
All agreements are not contracts.	All contracts are agreements.

Now that you know the difference between an agreement and a contract, dive into the essentials of a valid contract.

The essentials of a valid contract are given in section 10 of the Indian contract act, but there are a few essentials that are not given in the section but are required for a contract to be valid.

The following are the essential elements of a contract:

As given by section 10 of the Indian contract 1872

Not given by section 10 but are also essentials

As given by section 10 of the Indian contract 1872	***Not given by section 10 but are also essentials***
Agreement	Two parties
Free consent	Intention to create a legal relationship
Competency of the parties	Fulfillment of legal formalities
Legal object	Possibility of performance
Lawful consideration	Certainty of meaning
Not expressly declared to be void	-

The following are the essential elements of a contract as given by section 10 of the Indian contract act, 1972

1. Agreement:

an agreement is the first essential element of a valid contract.

1. Free consent:

two or more people are said to have given consent when they agree upon the same thing in the same sense. This can also be understood as the identity of minds in understanding the terms namely "Consensus ad idem". Without any coercion or undue influence.

Example: Jahnavi was warned by Kaivy that she would kill her if she didn't agree to sell her car. Because Jahnavi's consent was not freely given and the contract was made by coercion, it is invalid in this instance.

1. Capacity of the parties:

capacity to contract means the legal ability of a person to enter into a valid contract. Section 11 of the Indian contract specifies that every person is competent to contract who:

Is of the age of majority according to the law to which he is subject and,

Is of sound mind, i.e., should not be of unsound mind

There are 3 categories of unsound mind

I. Lunatic (Has phases of sound mind)
II. Idiot (Is dumb by birth)
III. Intoxicated person (a person who has consumed any substance that can cause intoxication)

Is not otherwise disqualified from contracting by a law to which he is subject.

A person competent to contract must fulfill all the above three qualifications.

Example 1: Anirudh at the age of 16, a minor, and Chetan a major entered into a mortgage agreement in which Anirudh pledged to pay back the money borrowed within a year with interest. However, Anirudh did not pay back the money as promised, and since their contract is void-ab-initio, Chetan cannot sue Anirudh for breach.

Example 2: Sujay, who is a person of unsound mind, and Srujana entered into a contract in which Sujay promised to buy Srujana 500 shares of the Cadbury Company for 2,00,000 ?. Sujay failed to do so even after receiving 2,00,000 ?, but Srujana cannot sue Sujay for breach of the contract because Sujay was not of sound mind at the time the contract was entered into.

Example 3: Siva was a convicted felon, yet deep entered into a contract of sale with him without being aware of this. In this case, Siva agreed to sell Deep an iPhone for 80,000 ?, and Deep paid Siva 80,000 ?, but Siva did not deliver the iPhone to deep. Deep cannot thus sue Siva for breach of contract because Siva is prohibited from entering into contracts under the law to which he is subject.

3. Consideration:

It is referred to as "quid pro quo" i.e., "something in return"

Example: Chanikya and Gokul made a contract wherein Chanikya will sell his snakes to Gokul for 1 lakh ?. So, in this contract between Chanikya and Gokul. Consideration for Chanikya = 1lakh ?

Consideration for Gokul = Snakes.

4. Lawful consideration and object:

The consideration and object of the agreement must be lawful.

Example 1: Samardtha rented a flat from Nikit for 1lakh ? on monthly basis to be paid. Consideration of Samardtha = flat, consideration of Nikit = 1 lakh, this is lawful consideration.

Samardtha rented this flat so he could make bombs inside the house. The object of the contract.

Therefore, it is not a valid contract.

Example 2: Anusha wants to sell her bike to Rohit; she wants Rohit to give her drugs in exchange for a bike. This is not a valid contract as this is unlawful.

5. Not expressly declared to be void:

A contract must not be expressly declared to be void for it to be a valid contract.

Example: Aryan made a contract with Ekansh a minor that Ekansh will pay 2000 ? to Aryan if Ekansh fails in his law exam.

This contract is expressly declared to be void as a contract with a minor is void-ab-initio.

The following are the essential elements of a contract that are not mentioned in a contract but are needed for the contract to be valid.

1. Two parties:

A contract requires the participation of at least two parties, one of whom makes the offer and the other who accepts it. Natural persons and other persons with legal existence both have the ability to enter into contracts.

Example: There must be two parties—a seller and a buyer—in order for there to be a sale contract. Since a single person cannot purchase his things, the vendor and the customer must be two separate individuals.

2. Parties must intend to create a legal obligation:

A contract must impose binding legal responsibilities on the parties. There is no contract between the parties and they are referred to as social agreements if they do not intend to generate legal responsibilities. Social agreements are not regarded as contracts.

Example: Vasantha promises her sister Karuna that she will give Karuna 50,000 ? if Karuna helps her complete an assignment. However, after Karuna assisted Vasantha with the assignment, Vasantha did not pay the promised 50,000 ?. As a result, Karuna is unable to sue Vasantha in court to recover the unpaid 50,000 ? because their agreement was of a social nature and there was no intention to establish a legal relationship. Karuna cannot, therefore, claim the 50,000 ?.

3. Other Formalities to be complied with in certain cases:

In the case of certain contracts, the contracts must be in writing, where ever there are formalities, we need to fulfill such formalities only then it will be a valid contract.

Example: Raju and Kamya entered into a sales agreement under which Raju was to deliver the guitar to Kamya. The contract's acceptance communication had to be made in writing, and it was. If the communication hadn't been made in writing, the agreement would have been null and void.

4. Certainty of meaning:

The agreement must be certain and not vague (or) indefinite.

Example: Karthik agrees to sell her blue color car to Varshini for Rs 6 lakhs. The agreement is not valid because there is uncertainty.

5. Possibility of performance of an agreement

The term of the agreement should be capable of performing. An agreement to do an act impossible in itself cannot be enforced.

Example: Vamshi agreed that he would take the 1 Cr and bring Sushant Singh Rajput to alive. The agreement can't be enforced as it is not possible to perform.

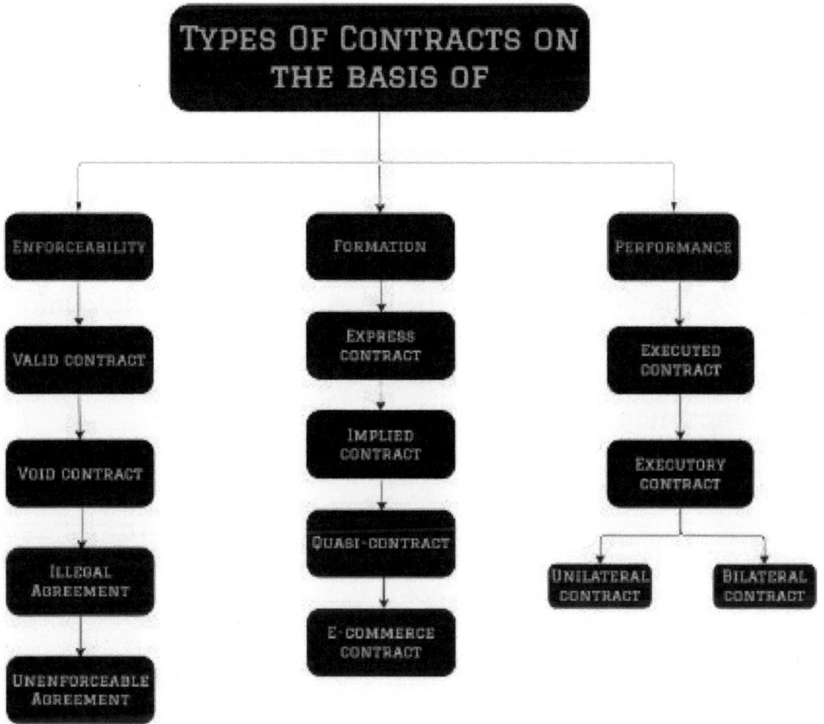

Types of contracts on the basis of

I. On the basis of the validity:

1. Validity contract: A valid contract is binding and enforceable. It includes every component that is necessary for a legal contract.
2. Void contact:

"A contract becomes void when it ceases to be enforceable by law," states the law.

Example: On September 30, 2020, Karthik plans to have S.P.B sing at his wedding. 25 September 2020. As S.P.B must arrive and carry out the contract, if S.P.B passes away, the agreement is worthless.

3. Voidable contract:

A contract is voidable if it can be enforced by the law at the choice of one (or) more party but not at the discretion of the other (or) other parties. Because this concern is not free, the agreed party receives an opinion.

Example: Rahul, was threatened with death if he did not give Kamya $10,000, so to preserve his life, he agreed to pay the sum. However, Rahul's fear was not legitimate, so he sought legal advice to nullify the contract.

Difference between void and voidable contract:

Void contract	Voidable contract
A contract ceases to be enforceable by law and becomes void when it ceases to be enforced.	An agreement that is enforced by law at this opinion there too, but not at the option at the other(s) is a voidable contract.
A contract becomes void due to a change in the law (or) change in circumstances beyond the compilation of parties.	A contract because of the voidable contract if the contract of a party was not free.
A void contract does not grant any right to any party.	The party whose content was not free has the right to resent the contract.
A void contract cannot be performed.	If the aggrieved party doesn't within a reasonable time, exercise his/her right to avoid the contract, any party can use the other claiming the performance of the contract.

4. Illegal contract:

Is a contract that the law forbids to be made. The court will not enforce such a contract but also the connected contracts will be disqualified. All illegal agreements are void, but all void agreements are not necessarily illegal. Kidnapping, murdering, smuggling of goods etcetera are all prohibited by law. Therefore, they are considered illegal contracts and can't be enforceable in the court of law, they are void contracts.

Example: vineesh made an agreement with Adithya to kill Karunya for a consideration of 50 lakh ?, in this case, if there is a breach, this contract will not be admissible in the court of law. As this contract is illegal in nature it becomes void and not enforceable by law.

Difference between Void and illegal contracts

Void agreement	Illegal agreement
A void agreement is not necessarily illegal	An illegal agreement is always void.
Not forbidden by law.	It is forbidden by law
Parties are not liable for any punishment under the law.	Parties to an illegal contract are liable for punishment.
It is not necessary that the collateral agreements to the void agreement are void. The collateral agreement may be valid.	Agreements collateral to the illegal agreements are always void.

5. Unenforceable Contract:

When a contract is valid in principle but is invalidated by certain technical factors, such as a lack of writing or a time limit, etc. It is referred to as an unenforceable contract since neither party/either party may bring a lawsuit against it.

Example: Rushikesh and Khushi entered into a contract of sale in which Rushikesh agreed to sell Khushi his iPhone 12 for 30,000 ?. Khushi communicated her acceptance of Rushikesh's offer by phone, and Rushikesh made his offer by email. If there is a breach of the contract, Rushikesh will be unable to pursue legal action because there is no valid evidence of acceptance, rendering the agreement Unenforceable.

II. On the basis of the formation of the contract:

1. Express Contract:
   It isn't composed of words. These agreements are made depending on the actions of the parties.
   Example: Thoshitha wrote a letter to Harini to buy her t-shirt for 10,000 ?. This is an express contract because it is made in writing.
2. Implied contracts:
   It isn't composed of words. These agreements are made depending on the actions of the parties.
   Example: Saniya visited a restaurant and placed a coffee order. There is an unspoken agreement that she will cover the cost of the coffee. As the proposition was accepted and agreed to through conduct.
3. Tacit contract:
   Contracts that are implied by the actions of the partics without any spoken or written form are known as tacit agreements. Tacit refers to silence. Example 1: withdrawing cash from the automated teller machine (ATM). Example 2: Purchasing any item from Vending machines.
4. Quasi-contract:
   the agreements established and signed as a result of the obligations the law imposes. Since there is no intention between the parties to enter into a contract, these agreements are not technically contracts.

Example: Ram Kumar unintentionally left his stuff on a bus. Ram Kumar and Anusha struck into a contract that requires Anusha to return the bag to Ram Kumar when Anusha discovered it in the bus due to a legal duty. Although the parties in this instance had no intention of entering into a contract, the law forced them to do so.

5. E-commerce Contracts:
   When a contract is entered into by two or more parties using electronic means, such as e-mails is known as an E-Commerce contract.
   Example: Komal buys a pair of earphones from amazon and enters into a contract of sale and pays the amount, this contract is called an e-commerce contract as the contract is made through electronic means.

III. On the basis of the formation of the contract:

1. Executed contract: A contract is deemed to be fully executed when both contracting parties have executed it.
   Example: Barre and Abhai signed a contract of sale in which Barre promised to sell Abhai his iPhone in exchange for one lakh ?. Barre received a one lakh ? payment from Abhai and gave him an iPhone. Given that both sides have kept their obligations, this agreement is termed executed.
2. Executory contract: a contract where a certain term still needs to be fulfilled in line with the terms of the agreement.
   Example: Poorvi decided to learn to drive. Sanjana said she will teach her to drive. Both parties are yet to do their performance. Sanjana still did not teach Poorvi. Poorvi is yet to pay the money, so it is an executory contract. As performance is remaining from both the parties.

a. Unilateral contract: It is a one-sided contract in which only one party has to perform the obligation.
   Example: Sanjana Taught Poorvi how to drive. Poorvi is yet to pay the cash. So as poorvi's performance is still outstanding. One of the parties is yet to perform their obligation in this case the contract is unilateral.
b. Bilateral contract: A contract where both parties are yet to perform their promise.
   Example: Varsha offered to paint Rahul's image. Rahul promised to pay ? 2000 for the painting. Both parties are yet to begin their performance, therefore. It is a bilateral contract.

<u>Offer/Proposal & acceptance</u>

Offer: When one person conveys to another that he is willing to act or refrain from doing something in order to gain the asset of the other person. He is said to make an offer.

Example 1: Venu offers to pay 5 lakhs for Kaara's car.

Example 2: Venu offers Kaara 5 lakh ? to not sell her car to anyone.

Essentials of an offer/proposal:

1. Promisor/offeror: a person making the proposal/offer is called "promisor" or "offeror".

   example:

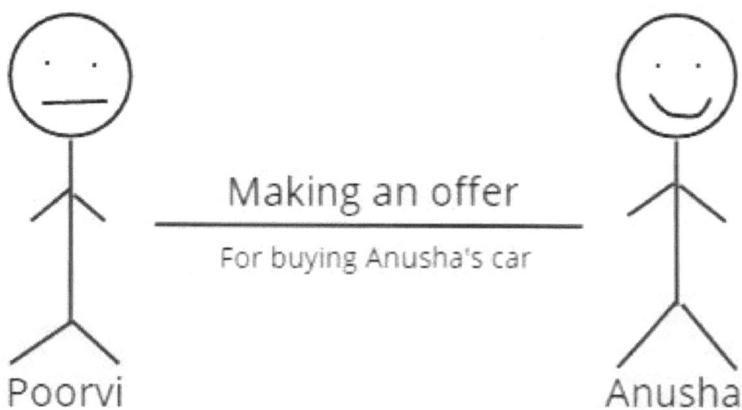

2. Acceptance: A valid offer requires the person offering it to convey his willingness "to do" or "not to do" something. An expression by itself does not represent an offer.

Example: Anirudh offered Satvika 2 lakh for her television; in this scenario, Satvika's readiness "to sell" or "not to sell" her television is insufficient; she must declare her willingness "to sell" or "not to sell" her television.

3. Positive or negative: An offer may be positive or negative.

Example 1: Rajamouli offered Prabhas a hero part in his film (positive) [to perform something].
Example 2: Prabhas stated that he will not act in any other projects other than Rajamouli's (Negative) [abstinence from doing something].

4. Assent: The offer must be made in order to get consent.

Example: if Anirudh says he wants to buy Satvika's iPhone for 1 lakh ?, that is an offer made in order to acquire assent; however, if he just says he wants to buy an iPhone from Satvika, that is not an offer made in order to obtain assent.

<u>Kinds of offer:</u>

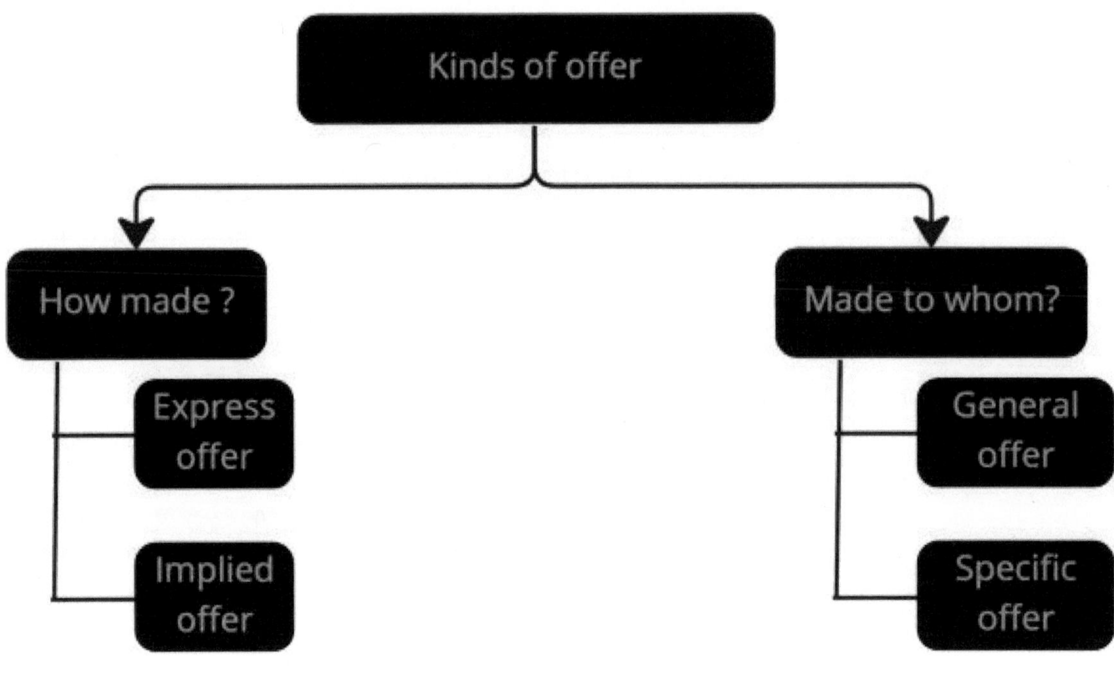

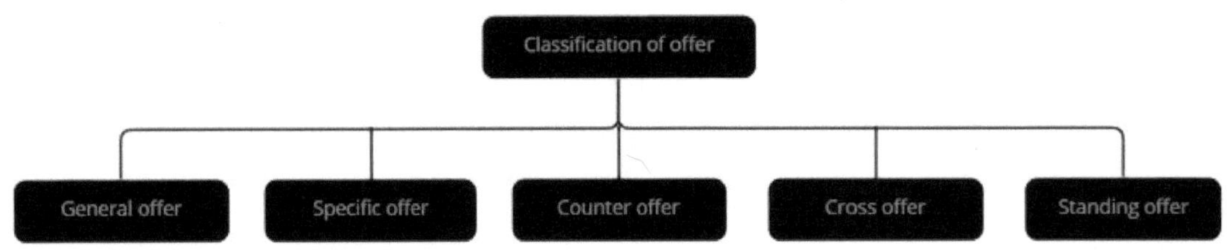

a. General Offer: It is an offer made to the public at large and hence anyone can accept and do the desired act.

Landmark case 1:

Carlill Vs Carbolic ball co. (1893)

Facts: In this case, Carbolic smokeball advertised in numerous publications that a $100 compensation would be granted to anyone who contracted influenza after using the carbolic smokeball company's smokeballs according to the specified directions. Mrs. Carlill, who used the smokeballs as directed by the firm, was facing influenza at the time. The corporation refused to compensate Mrs. Carlill, claiming that the offer was not made to women.

Judgment: The court ruled that because the offer was presented to the general public without any limits and conditions, the smokeball company was ordered to pay Mrs. Carlill $100.

Landmark case 2:
Lalman Shukla Vs Gauri Dutt

Facts: Gauri Dutt sent his servant Lalman to trace his missing nephew. He then announced that anybody who traced his nephew would be entitled to a reward of 500 ?. Lalman traced the boy in ignorance of the announced reward. Subsequently, when he came to know of the reward he claimed it, but Gauri Dutt refused to pay the reward to Lalman.
Judgment: The court declared that Lalman was not entitled to receive the reward as at the time of tracing the kid he was not aware of the reward, which signified that Lalman wasn't aware of the offer made.

b. Special/Specific Offer:
When the offer is made to a specific or an ascertained person, it's known as a special/Specific offer.

Example: Karthik contracted with Neha to deliver some goods. Before delivering the goods, Neha sold her business to Bhaskar. Now, Bhaskar delivered the goods to Karthik, it was held that Karthik is not liable to pay as there was no contract between Karthik & Bhaskar. Since it is a special offer only Neha could deliver the goods.

c. Counter Offer:
when the offeree gives qualified acceptance of the offer subject to changes and alterations in the original offer's terms, He is alleged to have counter-offered. A counter-offer is essentially a rejection of the previous offer. It is also known as conditional.

Example: we go to a vegetable vendor and enquire how much a 1Kg onion costs. It is said to cost 40. We settle for $30. This is referred to as a counter offer.

d. Cross Offer:
When two parties exchange identical offers while unaware of each other's offers, the offers are referred to as a cross offer. In such a circumstance, there is no binding contract because an offer made by one person cannot be regarded as acceptance of another's offer.
Example: Anjani sent Amrutha an e-mail offering her a motorcycle for 50,000. Amrutha called Anjana without knowing about the email and asked whether she could sell her motorcycle for 50,000. When Amrutha contacted Anjani and made the same/identical offer, it does not imply acceptance of Anjani's offer.

e. Standing/Continuing/Open Offer:
An offer that is allowed to remain open for acceptance over a period of time is known as a Standing/continuing/open offer.
Example: Big Billion Days, the offer made by Flipkart is an offer that stands open for a period of time.

Essentials of a valid offer:

i. It must be capable of creating legal relations
ii. It must be certain definite and not vague
iii. It must be communicated to the offeree
iv. It must be made with a view of obtaining the asset of the other party.
v. It may be conditional
vi. Offer shouldn't contain a term the non-compliance of which would amount to acceptance.
vii. The offer may be either specific or general
viii. Offer is different from a mere statement of intention, invitation to offer, a mere communication of information, and casual equity. A prospectus and advertisement.
ix. An intention to make an offer or to do business

x. A statement of intention and announcement

xi. Offer must be distinguished from an answer to a question.

Acceptance

as per Section 2(b):

when the person to whom the proposal is made signifies his assent thereto. The proposal is said to be accepted. The proposal when accepted, becomes a promise.

Relationship between offer and acceptance:

According to sir William Anson "Acceptance is to offer what a lighted match is to a train of gunpowder.

legal Rules regarding a valid acceptance

1. Acceptance can be given only by the person to whom the offer is made.
   · [Boulton vs. Jones (1857) → Special offer
   . [car till vs. carbolic Smoke Ball co (1893)] → general offer
2. Acceptance must be absolute and unqualified
   Case law 1-

   Neale vs. Merret [1930]

M offered to sell his land to 'N' for rupees 280. 'n' replied purporting to accept the offer but enclosed a cheque for Rupees 80 only. He promised to -pay the balance of 2 rupees 200 by monthly installments of rupees 50 each. It was held that N Could not enforce his acceptance because it was not an unqualified one.

Case law 2-

[Union of India vs. Bahulal AIR 1968 Bombay]

A offers to sell his house to B for rupees 100,000, B. replied. I can pay 80,000/- for it. The offer of 'A' is rejected by 'B' as the acceptance is not unqualified. B. however changes his mind and is prepared to pay rupees 1,00,000. This is also treated as a counter offer and it is up to A whether to accept it (or) not.

Case law 3 –

[Heyworth Vs Knight [1864]

A mere variation in the language not involving and difference in substance. wouldn't make the acceptance ineffective.

3. The acceptance must be communicated.

Case laws - [Brogden Vs Metropolitan Railway Co. (1877)]

B a supplier sent a draft agreement relating to the supply of coal to the manager of railway co. viz, Metropolitan railway for his acceptance. The manager wrote the word "Approved" on the same and put the draft agreement in the drawer of the table intending to send it to the company's so lictors for a formal Contract to be drawn up, by oversight the draft agreement remained in the drawer. Held, that there was no contract as the manager hadn't Commercial Communicated his acceptance to the supplier,

4. Acceptance must be in the prescribed mode.

Where the mode of acceptance is prescribed in the proposal, it must be accepted in that manner.

Example: Joshitha gave an offer to Mounika and Communicate that it should be accepted only through the email of the event. Mounika should accept through e-mail, as she couldn't see it failed, and there wouldn't be any contract.

5. Time: Acceptance must be given within the specified time unit if any, and if no time is stipulated, acceptance must be given within a reasonable time and before the offer lapse. what is reasonable time depending on the facts and circumstances of the particular case.

6. Mere silence not acceptance. Note: Unless the offeree has in any previous conduct indicated that his/her/their Silence is the evidence of acceptance.
   Case law - [Felthouse Vs Bindley (1862))

F offered to buy his nephew's horse mine at 730. The nephew did not reply to F at all.
He told his auctioneer, B to Keep the particular horse out of the sale of his farro stack as he invented to reserve it for his uncle. By mistake the auctioneer sold the horse. F' sued him for conversation of his property held, f' couldn't succeed at his nephew have not communicated the acceptance to him.

7. Acceptance can be through Conduct /implied acceptance.

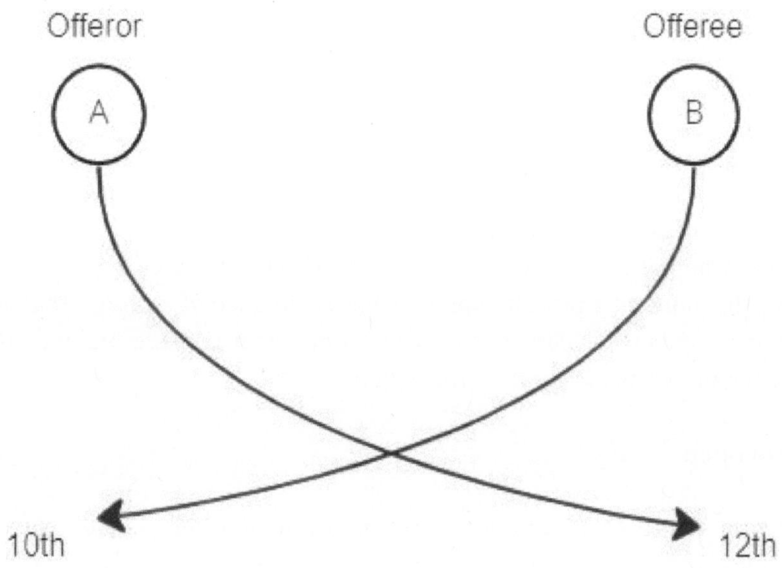

- Communication of offer and acceptance: -

The communication of offer is complete when it's to complete person to when it's made.

- As against the proposer: when it Is put in the course of transmission to him so as to be out of the power of the acceptor to Withdraw the same.
- As against the acceptor, when it comes to the knowledge of the propose

Communication of Special Conditions: Sometimes here are situation where there are contracts with special Condition. These special conditions are conveyed tacitly and the acceptance of these conditions are also conveyed by the offree again tacitly and the Acceptance of these conditions are also conveyed by the offree again tacitly or without him even realizing it.

Case law: - [Raipur transport (o. vs Ghanshyam [1956] A-Nag. 145]

A transport carrier accepted the goods for transport without any conditions Subsequently, he issued a circular to the owners of goods limiting his liability for the goods. In such a case, since the special Conditional were not communicated prior to the date of contract for transport, these were not binding on the owners of goods.

Case law: - (Carlill Vs Carbolic & Smoke ball co)

Mrs. Carlill was entitled to a reward of $1vo es she had performed the Condition for acceptance. further as the advertisement, "didn't require any

communication of Compliance of the Condition, it was not necessary to communicate the same. The court thus in the process laid down the following three important principles:

i. On, offer, to be capable of acceptance, must contain a definite promise by the offeror that he would be bound provided the terms specified by him are accepted:

ii. An offer may be made cither to a particular person or to the public at large, and.

iii. If an offer is made in the form of a promise in return for on act, the performance of that act, even without any communication thereof, is to be treated as an acceptance of the offer.

Revocation of offer and acceptance: -

i. As against the person who makes it, who when it a put into a course of transmission to the person to whom it is made so ad to be out of the person who makes it.
ii. As against the person to whom it is made, when it comes to his knowledge

   Note: - In English law, the moment a person expresses his acceptance of an offer, that movement the contract is concluded, and such an acceptance becomes irrevocable whether it is made orally or through the past In India law, the position is different as regards contract through past.

Modes of revocation of offer:

i. By notice of Revocation - The Communication d revocation of offer should reach the offeree before the acceptance is communicated.
ii. By lapse of time-

Example: Rohan gave an after to Sowmya which would be open for 6 days. If Sowmya doesn't accept within b days the offer comes to an end automatically.

iii. By non-fulfilment of Conditions precedent - where the offer requires that some conditions must be fulfilled before the acceptance of the offer, the offer lapses if it is accepted without fulfilling the condition.
iv. By Death or insanity
v. By Counter offer.
vi. By the non-acceptance of the otter according to the prescribed (or) usual mode.
vii. By Subsequent illegality

example: offer was made to be delivered on 20t October
The government declared on is of October that selling day is banned/ prohibited. Therefore, the offer automatically comes to end.

CHAPTER FOUR

CONSIDERATION

What is Consideration?

Section 2(d) defines: -

"When at the desire of the promisor, the promiser (or) any other person has done (or) abstained from doing or doesn't abstain from doing something, such as an act (or) abstinence (or) promise is Called consideration for the promise"

Analysis of the definition of Consideration:

1. Consideration is an act – doing Something:
2. Consideration is abstinence- abstaining from doing something.
   Example: - Husband and wife - diamond necklace.
3. Consideration must be at the desire of the promisor.
4. Consideration may move from promise (or) any other person.
   Example. - Paying my college fees by my parents.
5. Consideration may be past, present, (or) future

legal Rules Regarding Consideration: -

I. **Consideration must move at the desire of the promisor:**
   Consideration must be offered by the promise (or) the third party at the de ***(complete the word)*** or request of the promisor.

Example: - R saves s's goods from fire without being asked to do so. R cannot demand any reward for his services, as the act is voluntary.

I. **Consideration may move from promise (or) any other person: -**
   There can be a stranger to consideration but not a stranger to Contract.

III. **Executed and Executory Consideration: -**

Example: - Anusha pays 5000/- to Pavani and Pavani promises to deliver her a Cake within a month. In this case, Anusha pays the amount, whereas, Pavani merely makes a promise. Therefore, the consideration paid by Anusha is executed, whereas the Consideration promised by Pavani is executory

IV. **Consideration may be past, present, or future:**

Example: 'A performed some services to B' at his desire. After a week 'B' promises to Compensate A for the work done by him. It is said to be past consideration and 'A' can sue 'B" for recovering the promised money.

V. **Consideration need not be adequate: -**

It must be Something that the law would regard as having some value

VI. Performance of what one is legally bound to perform: -
Consideration must not be the performance of existing duty. Where a person promises to do more than that he is legally bound to de such a promise, it is a good Consideration.

VII. Consideration must not be unlawful, immortal, or opposed to public policy.

VIII. Consideration must be real and not Illusory
Example:

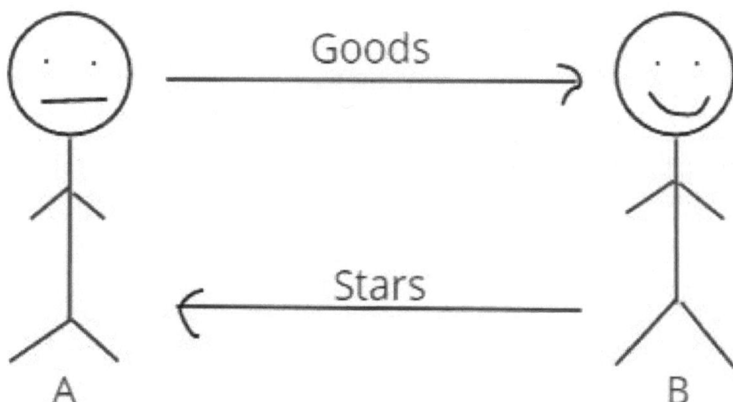

Here consideration of 'A' for giving good to B is not valid since it is illusory or not possible.

Suit by a third party to a contract: -

Only a person who is a party to a contract can use it. Stranger to a Contract cannot use Known as a "doctrine of privity at Contract" is, however, Subject to Certain exceptions. In other words, even a stranger to a contract may enforce a claim in the following cases:

1. In the case of trust: -

Example.: Anusha transferred her property to Disha to be held by Disha in trust for a benefit of Amrutha. In this case, Amrutha although not a party to the contract, can see for the benefit available to her the trust.

2. In case of family settlement:

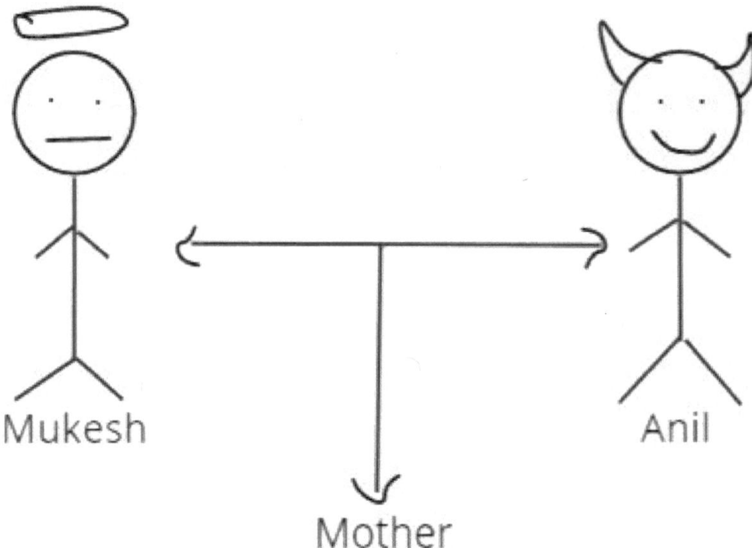

If any of her sons doesn't pay the money, she can file a case.

3. In case of assignment of a contract:

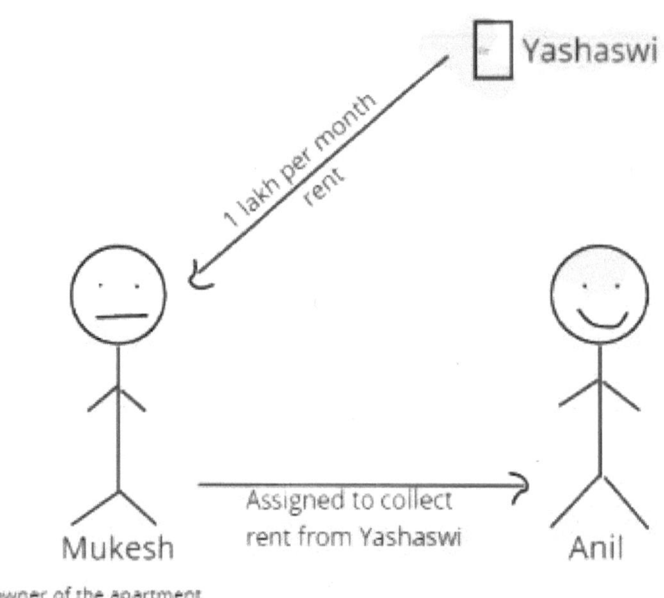

Here, Anil can file a case on Yashaswi If she doesn't pay rent even though she is not a party to the contract.

4. In the case of certain marriage contracts/ arrangements:

Here (alpha), and (beta) can file case on 'M' (or) 'A' they don't take care at them even though they are not a party to a contract.

5. Acknowledgement/ ***Estoppel:***

Case i.

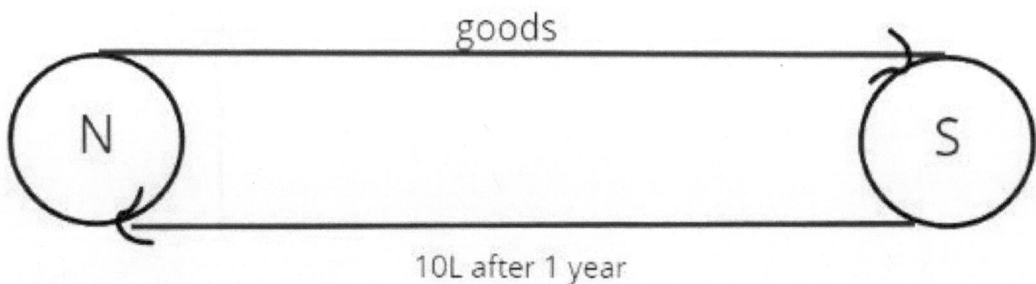

Case ii.

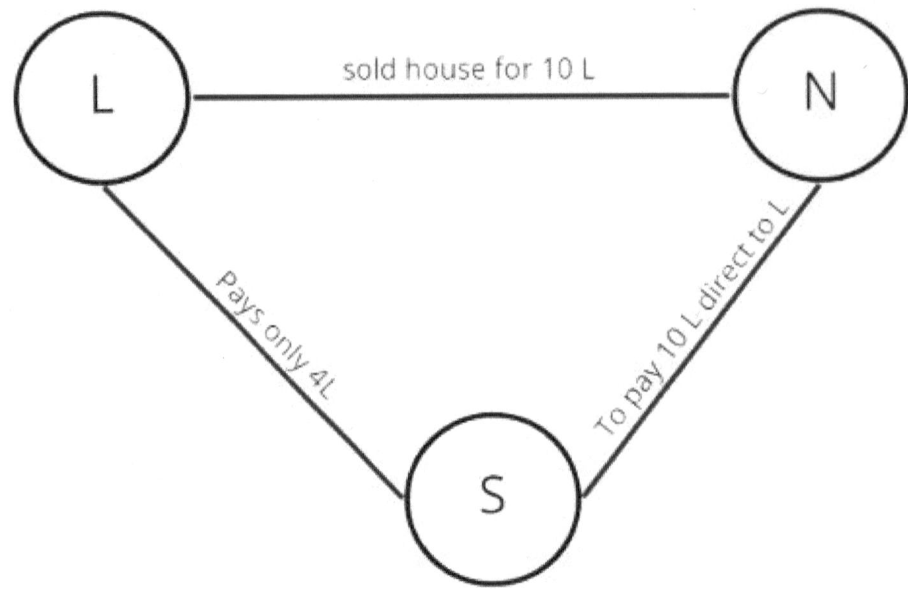

Here Lahari(L) can file a suit against Samartha(S) even though. Samartha is not a party to the contract.

6. In the case of a Covenant running with the land:

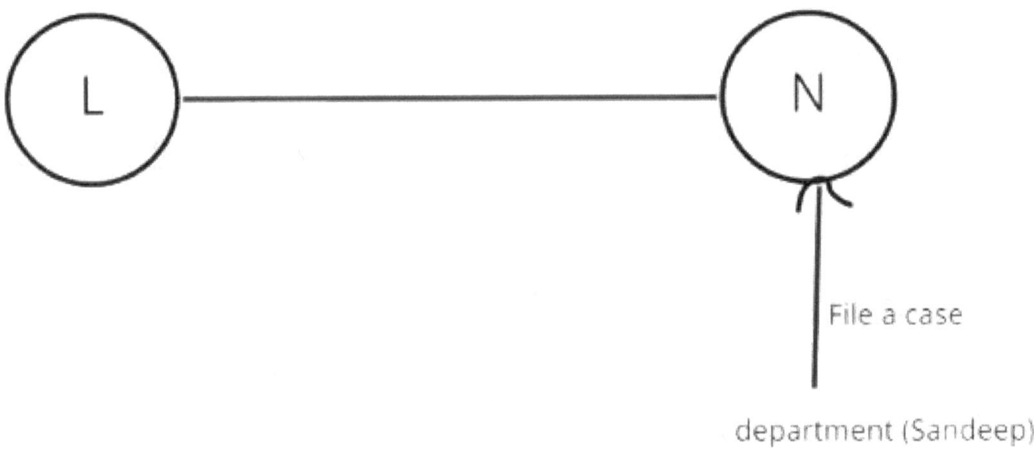

Here, even though the Contract is between Lahari and Nikit for not given paying tax [property tax] despite being a third party.

7. Contracts entered into through an agent:

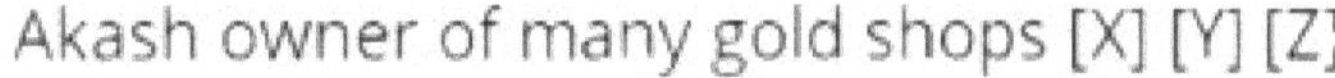

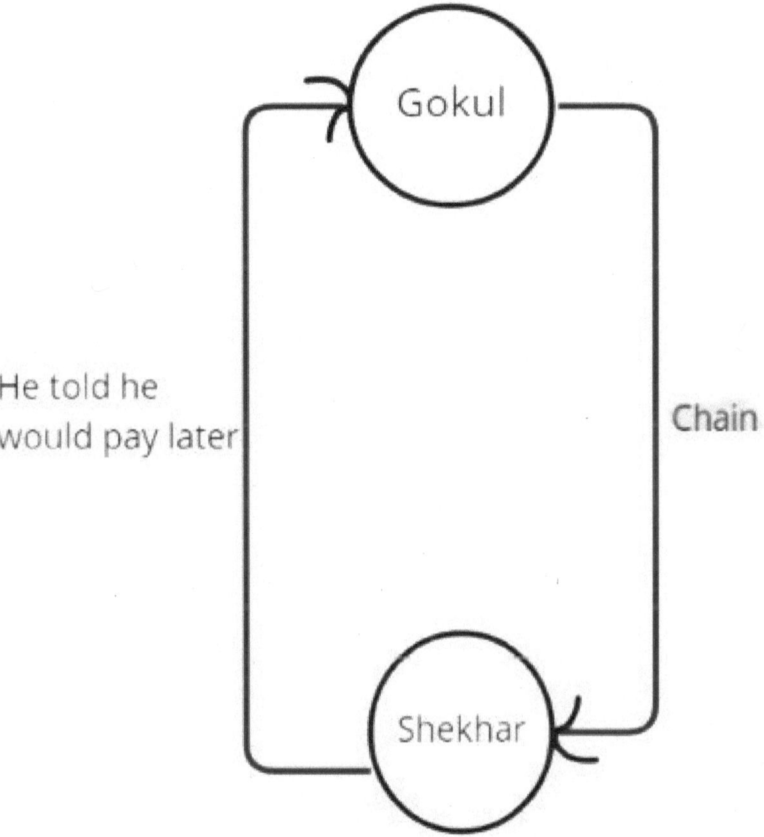

Here, Aakash can file a suit on Shekar if Shekar, doesn't pay money within money within a month despite being a kind person.

<u>Validity of an agreement without Consideration: -</u>

1. No Consideration = No Contract
2. But in the following cases, the agreement though made without Consideration I

   still valid. The following cases are:

1. Natural Love and affection:

   Conditions to be fulfilled:

a. Must be in Writing
b. There should be relationship between the parties in the Contract
c. It must be registered under law
d. There should be love and affection between parties.

example

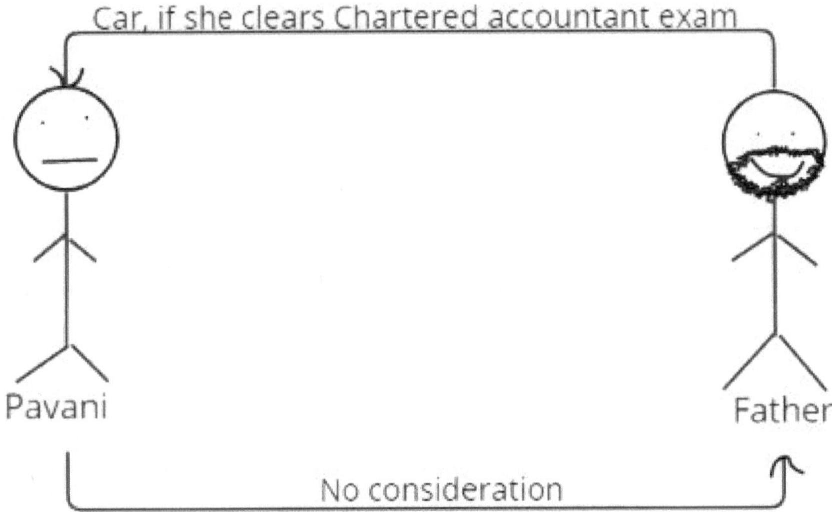

2. Compensation for past voluntary services:

   Conditions to be followed: -

a. The Services must have been done voluntarily:
b. Services: Rendered for the promisor
c. Promisor must be in existence at the time when services are rendered.
d. Promisor - Intends to Compensate for the Voluntary service

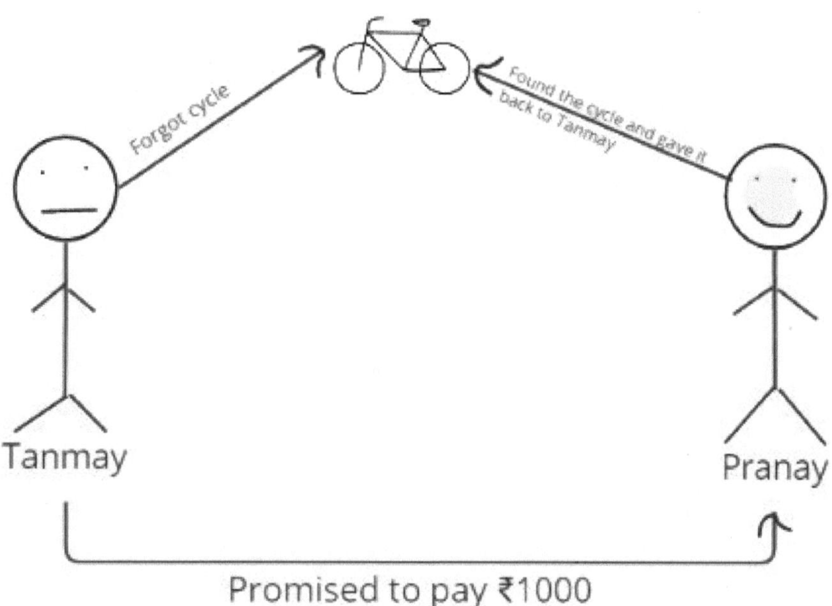

3. Promise to pay Time barred debt:

   Conditions are to be followed:

a. In Writing
b. limitation is defined & Expressed (lakh Rs)
c. Promise is signed by Promisor(M), 'V' Didn't file a case within 3years=Time barred debt.
d. Debt is time-barred

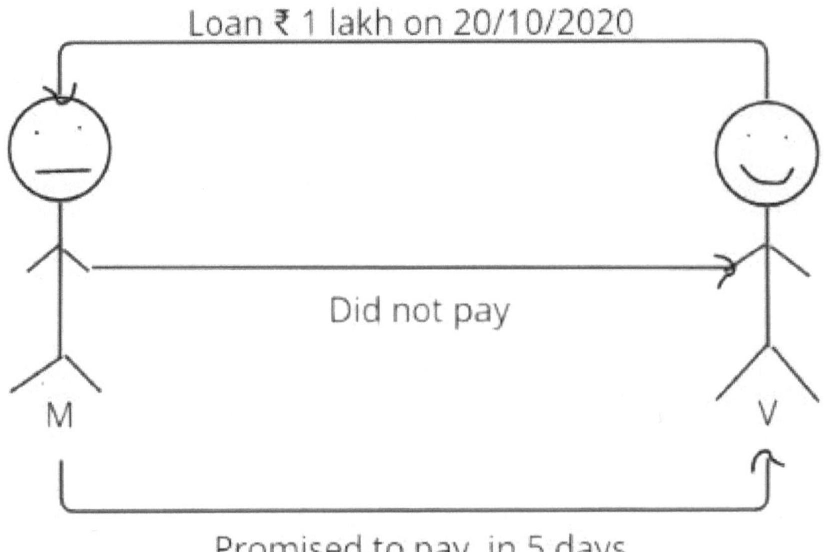

4. Agency:

   In Agency: - Even if there is no consideration still it is a Contract

5. Completed Gift:

   Even though ownership is transferred without Consideration it is still a valid Contract in the Case of gifts. 'K' Cannot go & take back the gift given later.

6. Bailment:

   No Consideration - there is a contract:
   A - has Consideration
   M - No Consideration

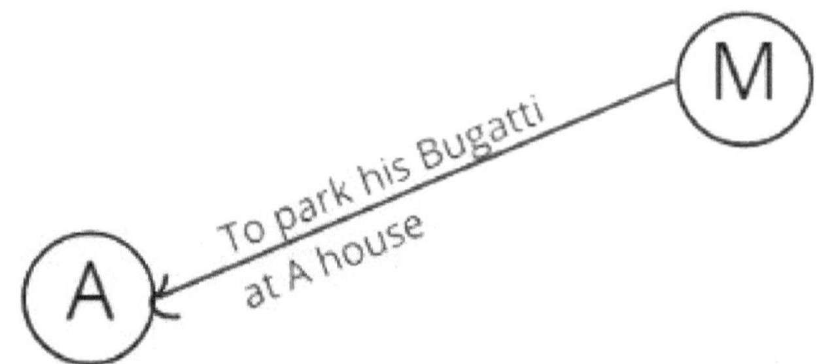

7. Charity:
   The voluntary giving of help, typically in the form of money, to those in need.

CHAPTER FIVE

OTHER ESSENTIAL ELEMENTS OF A CONTRACT

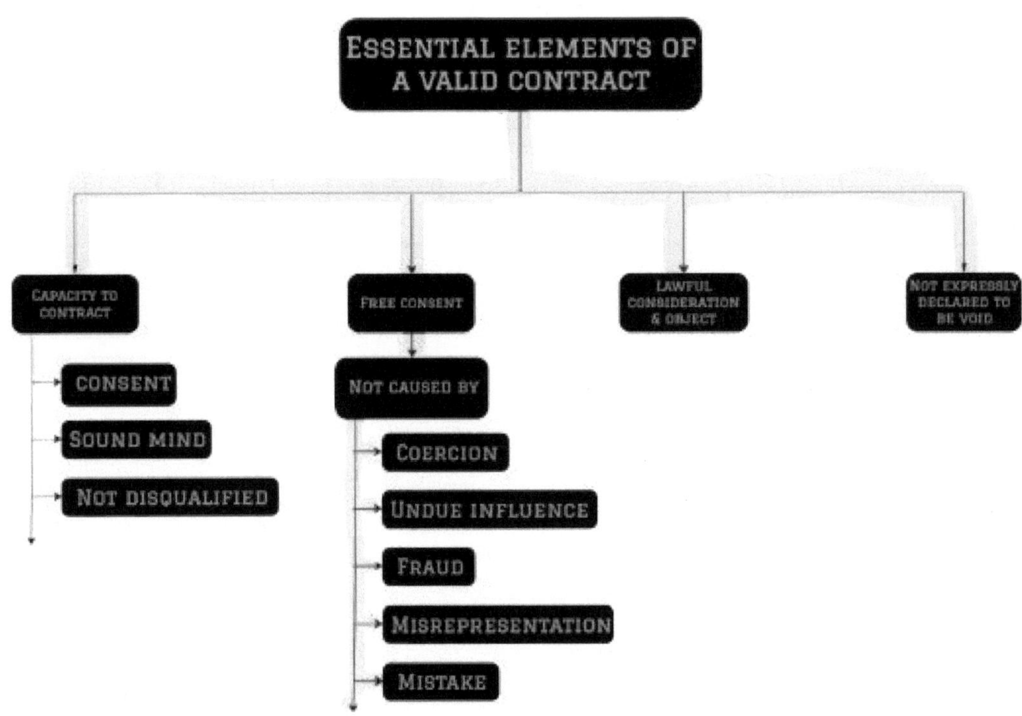

Capacity to contract

Who is Competent to contract (sec 11)

Every person is Competent to Contract who is of the age of majority according to the law to which he is subject, and who is of sound mind and is not disqualified from Contracting by any Law to which he is subject"

Age Of Majority:

A person is a major once the person attains 18 years of age

Law relating to Minors agreement / Position of Minor:

1. **A contract made by or with a minor is void ab-initio.**

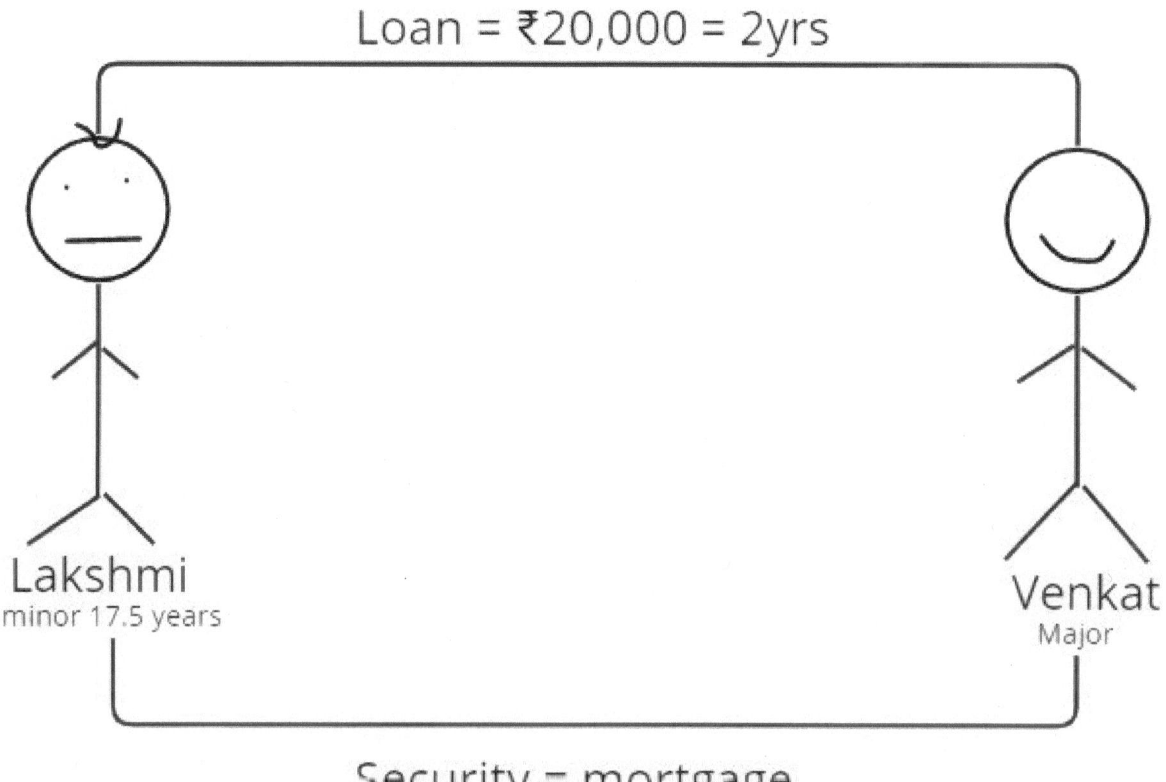

A minor is not Competent to Contract and any agreement with or by a minor Is void from the very beginning
Case law 1-
(Mohiri Bibi vs Dharmo das Ghose (1903))

It was held that a mortgage by a minor was void and B was not entitled to repayment of money.

1. **No ratification after attaining Majority:**

Example: X, a minor makes a promissory note in the name et Y. on attaining majority, he cannot ratify it and it he makes a new promissory note which he executed after attaining majority is also void being without Consideration.

3. **Minor can be a beneficiary or can take benefit out of a contract**

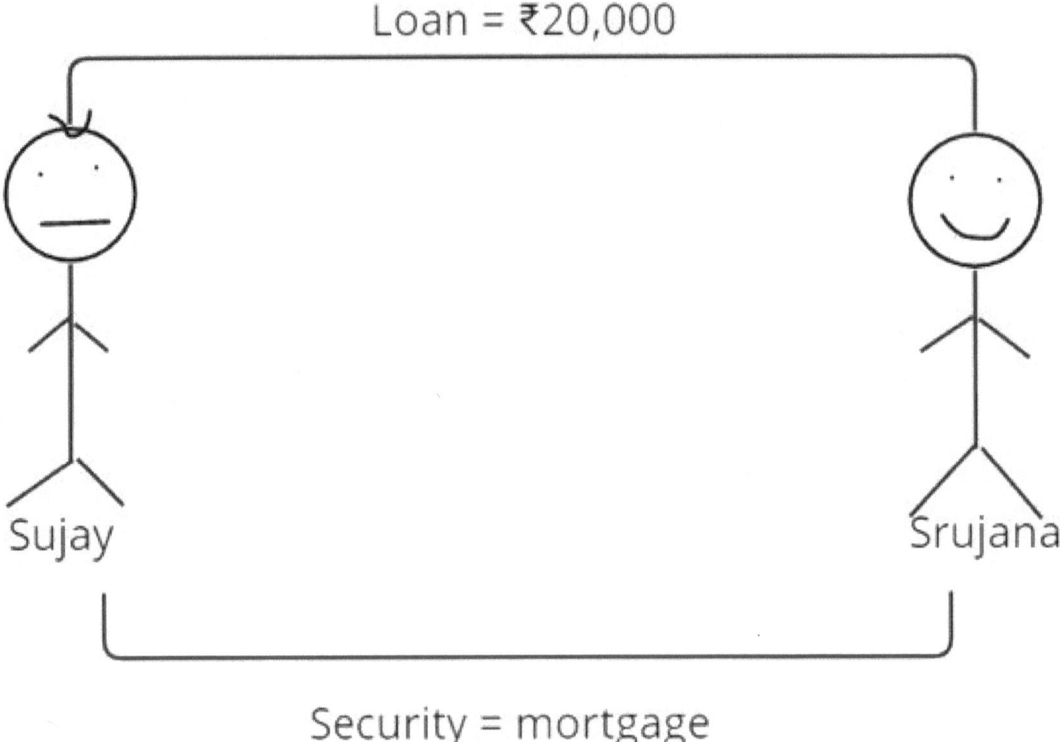

Minor -> protect

A Mortgage was executed in favour of a minor, Held, he can get a Decree for the enforcement of the mortgage.

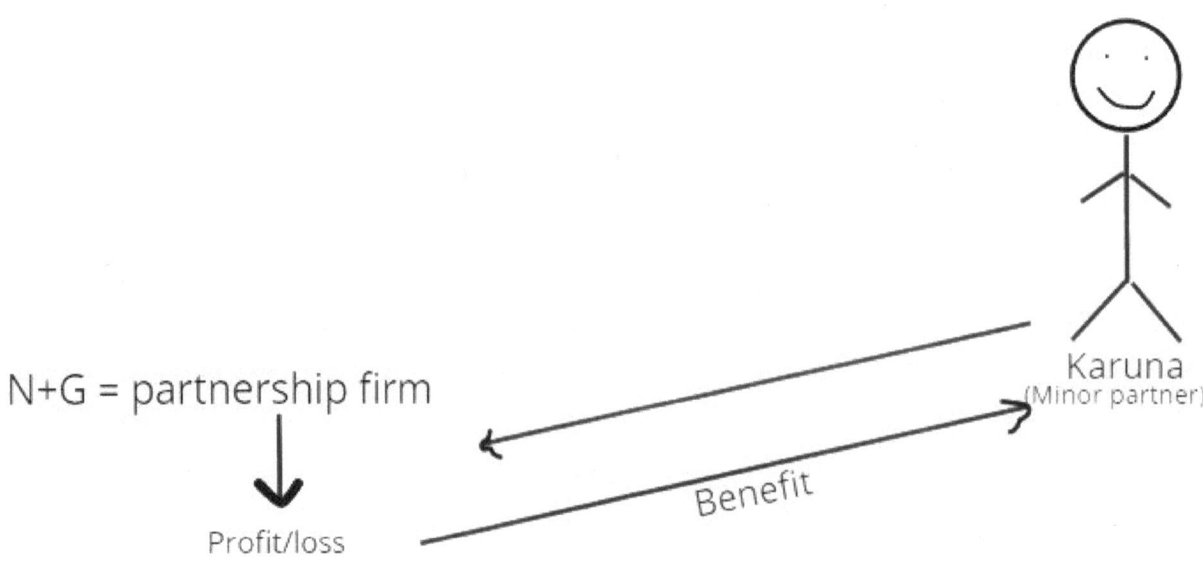

A minor cannot become partnership firm. However, he may with the consent of all the partners, be admitted to the benefits of a partnership.

4. **A minor Can always plead minority:**

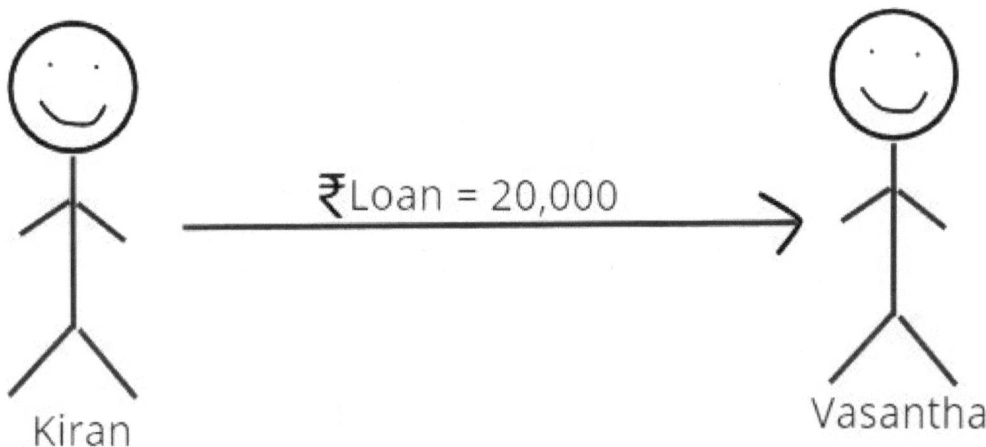

Minor can be allowed to plea his minority in defence even if he entered into a contract by falsely representing that he is a major.

5. **Liability for necessaries:**

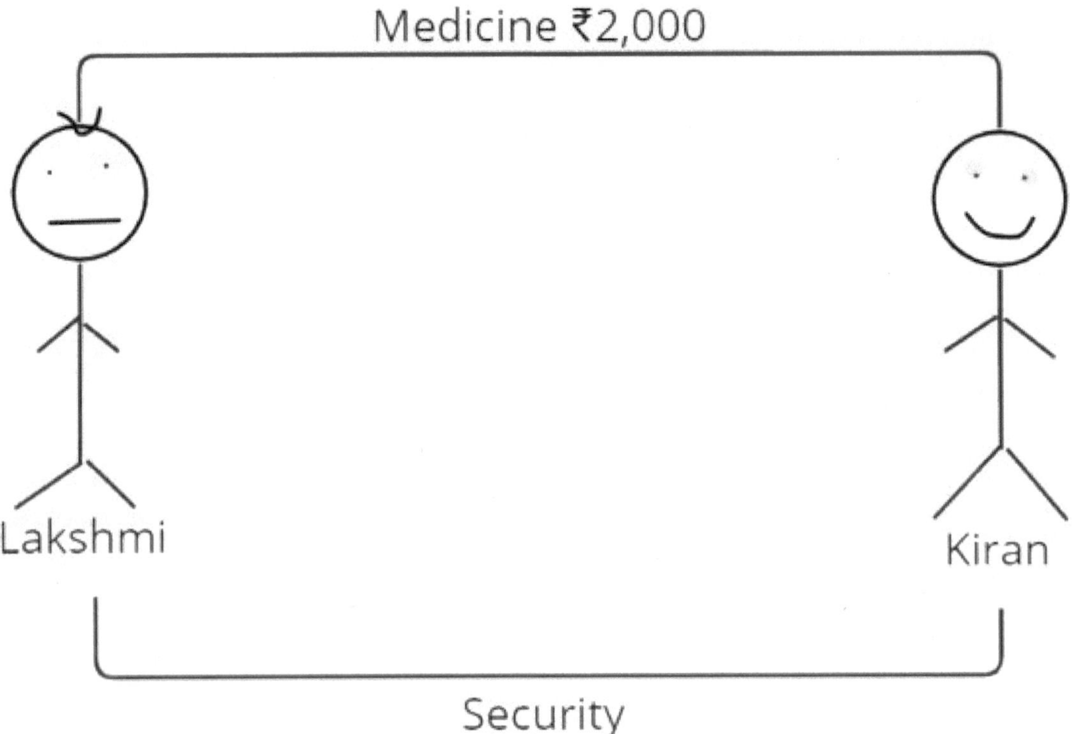

I. Property = 25,000
II. Diamond = Not necessary
III. SRK Son -» Car: Necessary status

It is legal to supply minors with necessities. The minor has no personal obligations, only his property is on the table.

There are two requirements that must be met in order for the minors' estate to be held liable for necessities:

a. The contract must be for the good's reasonable necessities for his support in the station in life.
b. The minor must not already have an adequate amount of these necessities. The standing of the minor in life is key to the entire issue. The criterion is use rather than adornment.

6. **Contract by Guardian - how far enforceable:**

Under certain conditions, a guardian may engage into a legally binding contract for the benefit of the child; these contracts will be legally binding and enforceable by the minor.

-> Immovable property = sanction of Court

7. **No specific Performance:**

8. **No insolvency:**

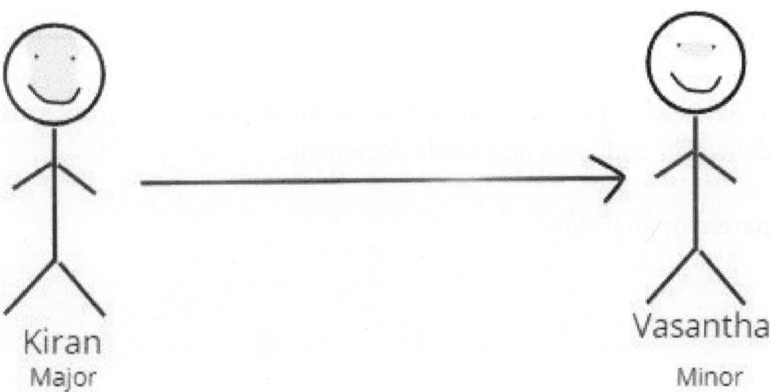

Insolvency means state of being unable to pay the debts by them.

9. **Partnership:**

He may form a partnership, in which case he won't be responsible for any losses and will only be allowed to profit from it.

10. **Minor can be an agent:**

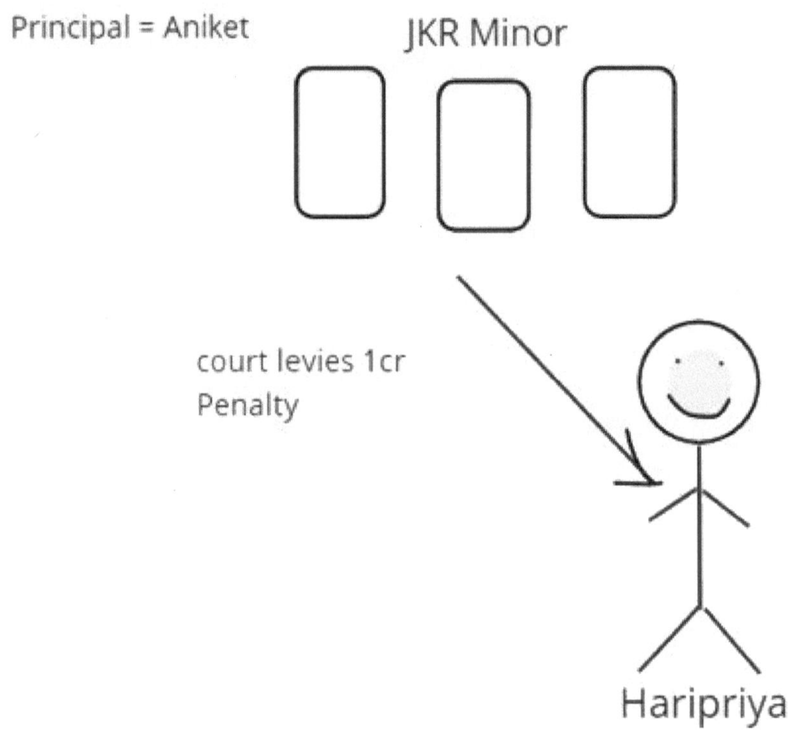

can serve as an agent. But he won't be held responsible for his actions by his principal. A minor is not personally liable when they draw, deliver, or endorse a negotiable document.

11. **Minor cannot bind parent or guardian:**

12. **Joint Contract by Minor and Adult:**

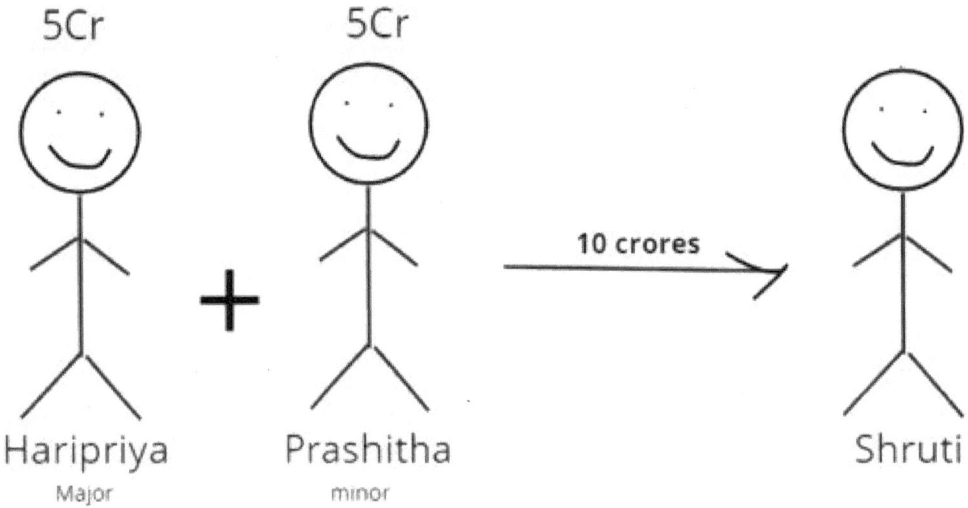

In this scenario, the adult and not the minor will be listed on the contract.

13. **Surety for a minor:**

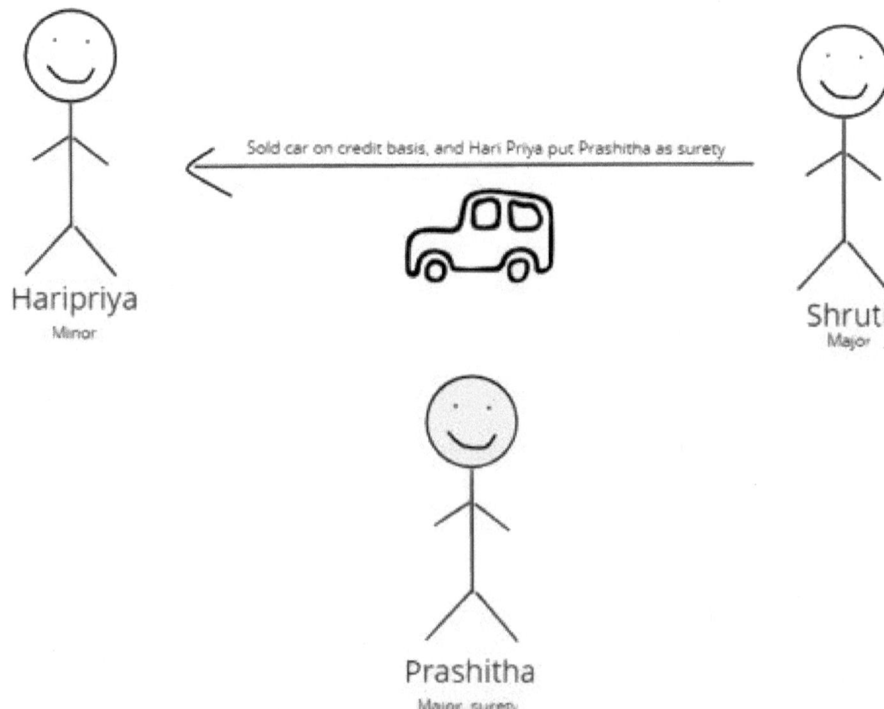

When an adult acts as a surety for a juvenile in a guarantee contract, the adult is liable to the third party since there is a direct contract between the surety and the third party.

14. **Minor as a shareholder:**

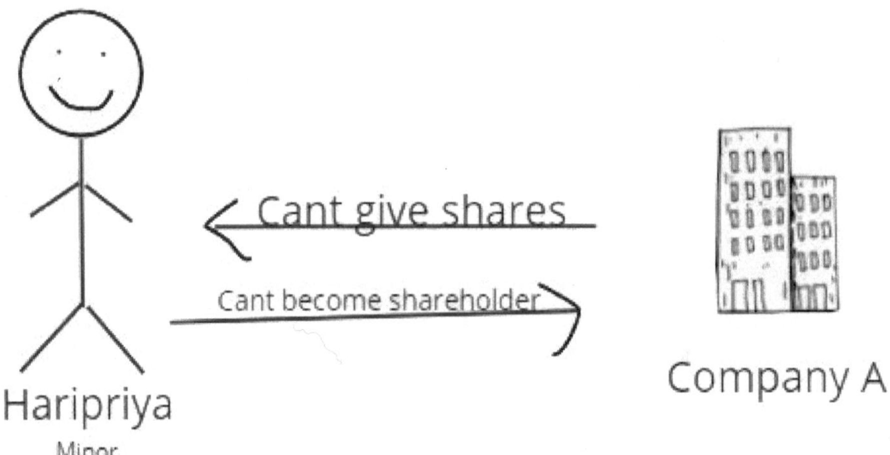

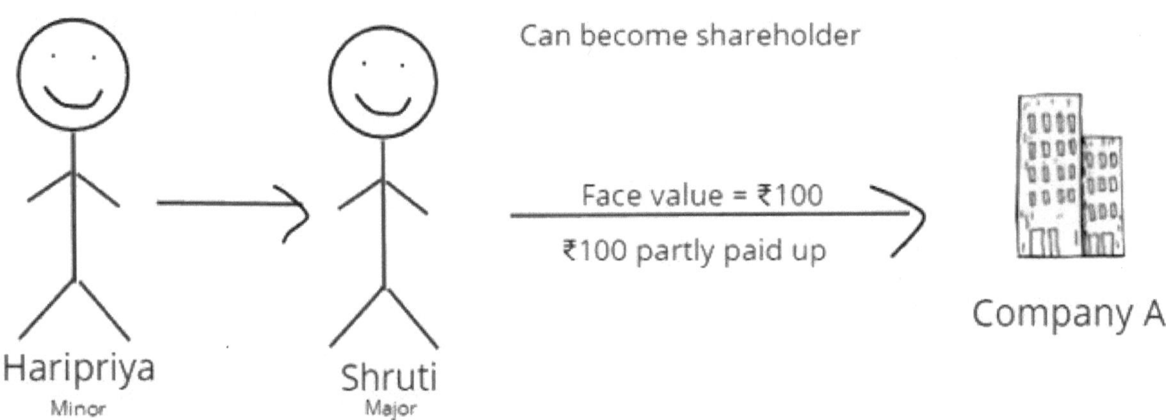

Enter Caption

I. Fully paid up
II. Guardian/ Parent

A minor who is unable to enter into a binding contract cannot own stock in the company. However, a minor acting through his legal guardian becomes a shareholder by transfer of transmission of fully paid shares to him. If by mistake he accidentally becomes a member, the firm can revoke the transaction and erase his name from the register.

CHAPTER SIX

PERFORMANCE OF A CONTRACT

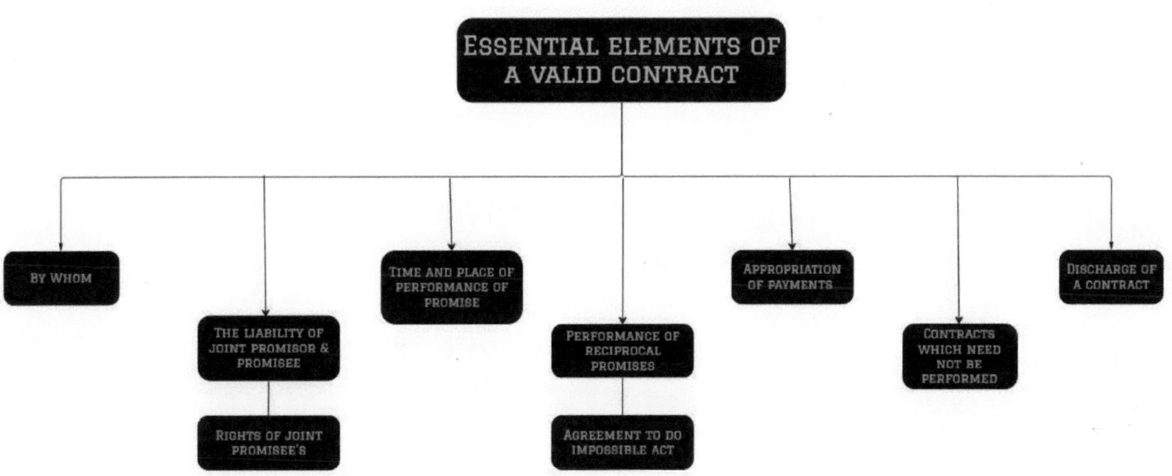

Obligations of Parties to Contracts

A contract owes its promises to the parties, who have a responsibility to fulfil them.

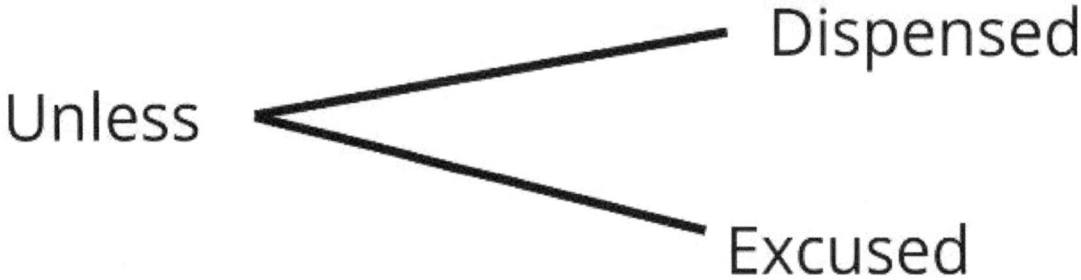

Example:

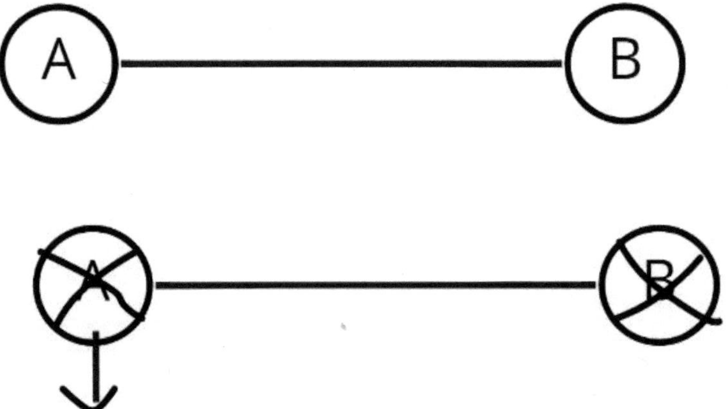

miro

If in The Contract, its written that /given that

- The legal representatives Would not perform

- If A dies, the Contract would be performed by A's friend c, then legal representative will not perform.

Effect of Refusal to accept offer of performance (Section 38)

- When a promisor offers to fulfil a promise and another offer to fulfil the promise is rejected, neither the promisor nor his rights under the Contract are affected by the other offer's failure to be fulfilled.
-
- Every such offer must meet the following requirements:
- • It must be unconditional;
- • It must be made at the appropriate time and place, and in circumstances that give the person to whom it is made a reasonable opportunity to determine that the person making it is able and willing there and then to do everything he is obligated to do by his promise to do It.
- The promise must have been made in order for the offer to deliver anything to the promise. a chance to reasonably determine if the thing being given is the thing to which the promisor is obligated due to his commitment to deliver it. The legal ramifications of making an offer to just one of numerous joint pledges are the same as making an offer to them all.

Effect of refusal of party he performs wholly (section 39)

If a party to a contract refuses to perform or makes it impossible for him to fully fulfil his promise, the contract may be terminated unless he has expressly expressed his agreement to continue it through words or actions.

By whom A contract may be performed (section 40, 41 & 42)

Promiser himself:

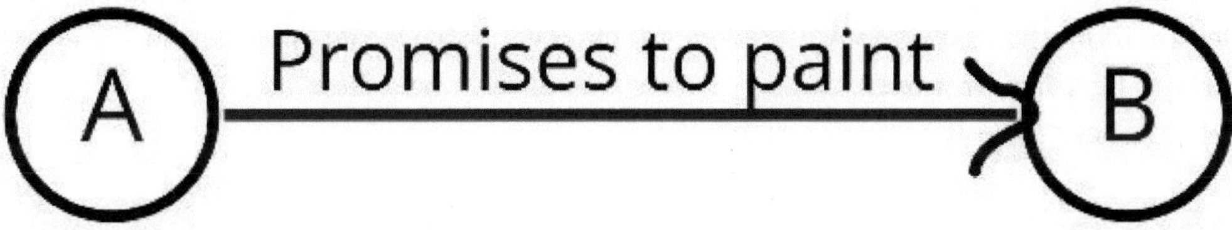

miro

but A dies, but no one can perform it.

Agent A can employ an agent to perform it.

Legal representatives:

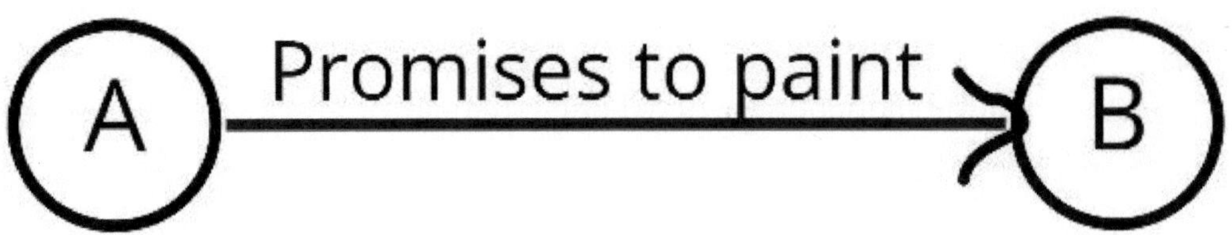

A has to perform can't ask another painter, If A dies, contract can't be enforced by anyone other than LR.

Third person:

A is the main barber but B the assistant cuts hair and takes moneyC, then C doesn't have to tell A

Joint- promisors:

When promise is made jointly, it should be fulfilled jointly.

A B C pays D

So, his Legal Representative will join B&C and fulfil, if Then their Legal representative will perform.

Distinction between Succession, and assignment

Succession: If assets are more than liabilities, A>L then pay all the liabilities and keep the assets.

and

Assignment: If liabilities are more than assets L>A, then give off assets and discharge liabilities

Effect of Refusal of Party to perform promise:

The person who was wronged has the following two rights:

a. to terminate the contract
b. to indicate by words that he is interested in its continuance

- denotation of joint liabilities:

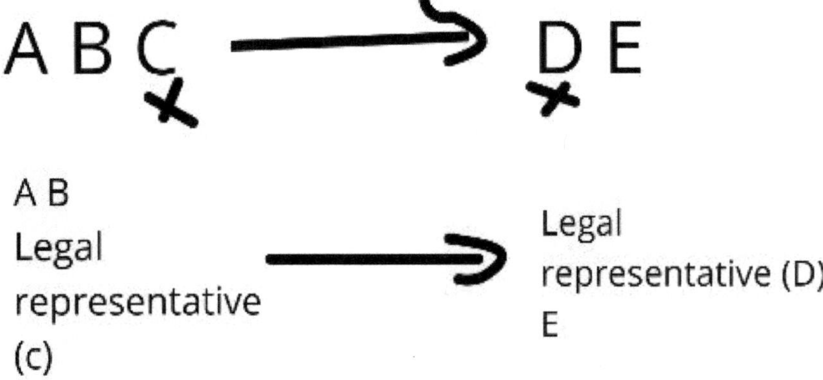

• In a joint pledge, their legal representation following the passing of either of them. group together to pay off the debts.

• In a joint promise, the promise may obligate any one or more of the joint promises in the absence of specific agreement to the contrary.

B pays 3 lakhs to JKR and then asks A&C 1 lakh each as he paid on their behalf.

- sharing of loss by default in contribution if anyone of two promisors make default in such concentration, the remaining joint Partners will bear the loss in equal shares.

Liability of joint promisor & promisee

- Effect of release of one joint promiser

Example: *Rohan, vidya, Vishnu -> JKR*
Then JKR released Rohan (Rohan shouldn't pay JKR) But Rohan should pay vidya & Vishnu

  - When two or more people make a joint promise, the promisee's release of one joint promisor does not release the other joint promisors or release the joint promisor(s) in question from liability to the other joint promisor(s) or promisee(s).
  - Right of Joint Promise: Unless a contrary intention is evident, a promise given to two or more people jointly is enforceable.

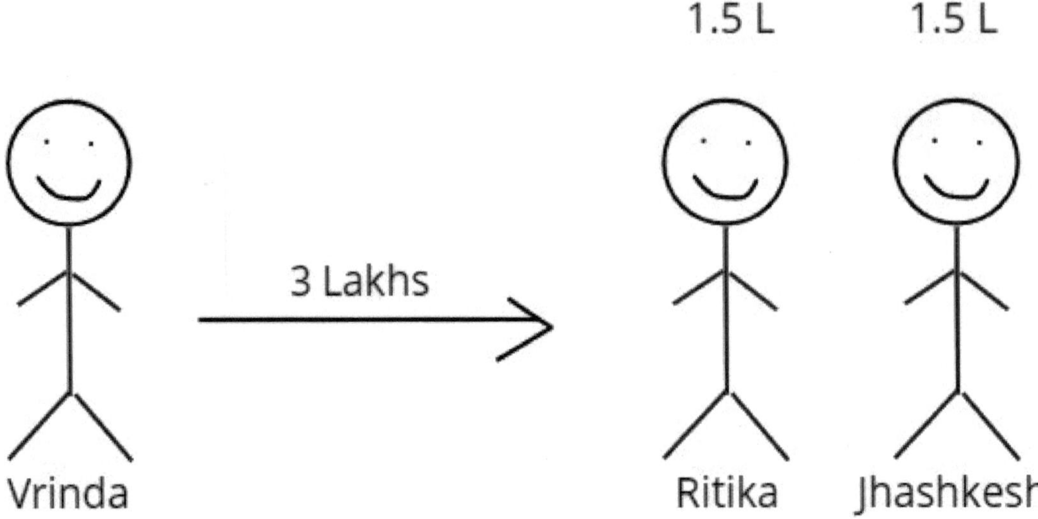

Vrinda told Ritika and Jhashkesh, she'll repay them the money he lent and if they die it goes to the Legal representative.

Right to demand performance under the terms of the agreement. rests, with them after death or anything, during their existence.

Time and place for performance at the promise

1. No application is required, and no deadline is given for the promise's performance. when no specific time is given. The promise must be made in a timely manner.
2. Where a time is stated and no application is required, the location where the promise will be fulfilled - section47. If no location is stated, the performance must take place at a reasonable location and the designated time, with a reasonable location being a place of business or a location where the other party is frequently available.
3. When a promise is requested to be carried out on a specific day and at the appropriate time and location, it is the promisee's responsibility to do so during regular business hours.
4. A location where a promise will be fulfilled where no application is required and no specific location has been designated.

When no location is specified, a reasonable location should be determined and the promise will be carried out there. Performance -> no app/place -> then reasonable place

1. Performance in manner or at time prescribed or approved by promisee - A promise will be performed in any way or at any time approved by the promisee.

Performance of reciprocal promise

1. Promises are not legally obligated to carry out unless a counterparty commitment is ready and willing to do so. When there is a contract, reciprocal promises must be kept.

Example: Akanksha sold goods to Bindu and Bindu should pay on delivery. A need not go deliver until B is ready and is willing to pay.

2. The sequence in which reciprocal commitments must be fulfilled is important since some contracts require it.

For instance, if you buy a plane ticket and then decide not to take it, the plane will still arrive at your workplace and you will still have to pay. Given the nature of the transaction, the contract should be carried out.

3. If a contract involves reciprocal promises and one of the parties prevents the other from keeping his promise, the party who prevented the event on which the contract was to take effect is liable.

Example: Mr. Abhai has to get his air conditioner repaired and Mr. Bala has to perform the repair. Mr. B - has to repair AC Mr. B comes to A's house and asks for opening the door to perform the repair but Mr. A wasn't opening the door.

4. The impact of a breach of that promise that should be fulfilled first in a contract with reciprocal commitments (section 54)

Example
So 'S' can complain that cause of his mistake, he is not able to perform need compensation when the promises are reciprocal & dependent it the promisor who has to perform his promise, before the performance of the other's promise fail to perform, he cannot claim performance of the others promise, is liable for compensation

5. Effects of failure to perform a time fixed in a contract in which time is

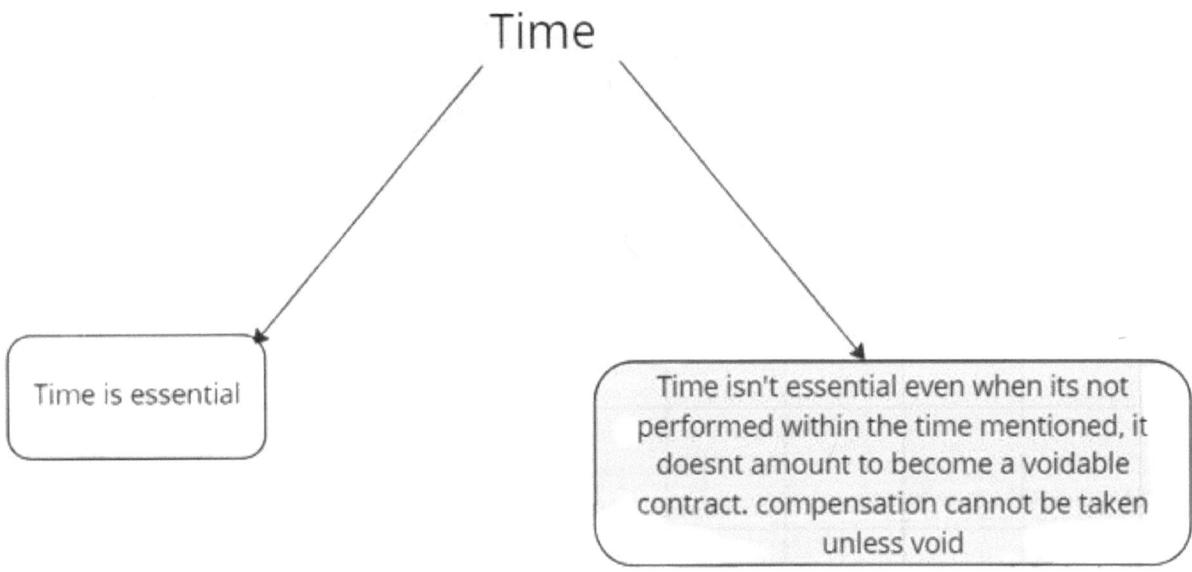

6. Agreement to do impossible Act

   an agreement to do an impossible act itself is void

a. Contract to do act after becoming impossible- (initially impossible)
b. Compensation for loss through nonperformance of act Known impossible (subsequent impossibility)

a. Initial impossibility

   Not everyone is aware that it's impossible to perform

I. If– Known To the parties
II. If known to the promisor only Promisor Knows but promisee agreed.

   Promisee is entitled to claim compensation for any less he suffered for im-performance.

b. Subsequent impossibility

It becomes Impossible by an unexpected event or change et circumstances beyond contemplation of parties ***A weds B and B becomes insane so A doesn't marry B.***

7. Reciprocal promise to do certain things that are legal and also some other things that are Illegal

- when a promise is reciprocated
- The first condition is valid
- The Second condition B void

Example) A sells house to B for 50,000 rupees is valid,
But B using that house as a gambling space for which he pays 75,000 then the contract is not valid.

8. As an alternative, instead of one branch being prohibited in this situation, only one branch can be enforced. ***A pays 1lakh to B Wherein B may*** deliver rice then contract is legal and valid or opium then contract is illegal and void.

APPROPRIATION OF PAYMENTS

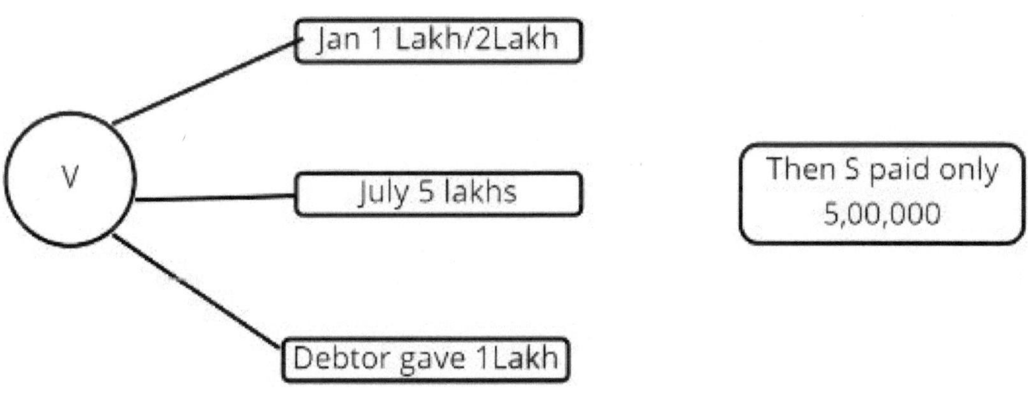

Case (1): when the debtor makes a payment, indicates the details of the payment to be as per the debtor's choice.
Case (2): when the Creditor doesn't mention the debt
Case (3): The payment shall be applied in the discharge of the debts in the order of time if neither party makes any acceptable representations regarding it. If the obligations are equal in standing, the payments must be applied in a proportionate manner to discharge each.

E.g., If neither Vasantha nor the creditors apply the payment received then it should be applied in the payment which came in the Earliest in this case it should be applied for January payment.

Contracts, which need not be performed - with the consent of both the parties.

1. Effect of novation, rescission and alteration of contract (section 62)

If the parties to a contract. agree to substitute a new contract for it or to rescind a alter it the original contract need not be performed,

a. Effect of Novation:

The parties to a contract may substitute a new contract for the old contract, old contract is discharged & consequently it need not be performed. New contract is substituted for it either between the same parties or between different parties

b. Effect of rescission:

when the parties to a contract agree to rescind it, the contract need not be performed. Only the old contract is cancelled & no new contract comes to exist in its place.

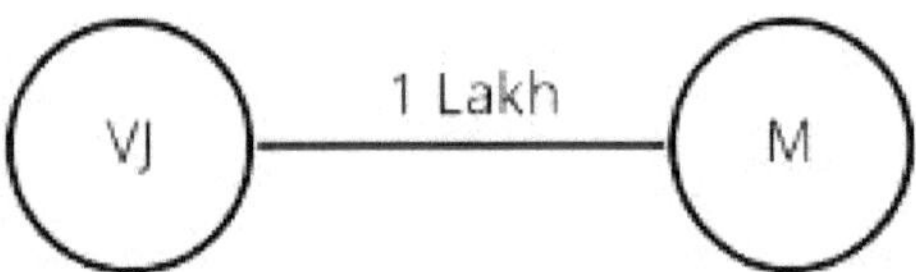

J&M both mutually agreed to cancel the contract

c. effect of alteration of Contract

where the parties to a contract agree to alter it. the original contract is rescinded, with the result that it need not be performed. The terms of contract may be -so altered by mutual an agreement that the alteration may have the effect of substituting a new contract for the old one

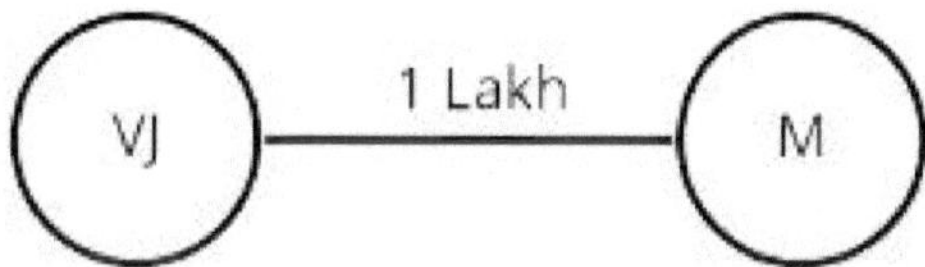

The terms & conditions between J& M have been changed so that old terms & conditions need not be performed.

2. Novation and alteration:

Novation means substitution of an existing contract with a new one
(ii) Promise may waive or remit performance of promise:
Every promisee may dispense with, in part, the performance of the promise made to him, or may extend the time for such performances may accept instead of any satisfaction which b.

Rohan has agreed to take this in full satisfaction, Now Vishnu need not pay the other 5 lakhs:

(iii) Benefit of Restitution a Voidable Contract A voidable contract may be cancelled at the discretion of the party with the authority to do so. If he obtained any benefits under the contract, he was required to return those benefits to the source.

Rohan's land is 5 lakhs, but, shiva and don coerced Rohan an took the land in exchange of an iPhone worth 1 lakh rupees.

1. Later on, Rohan sold the land to Vasantha
2. Since the initial contract is voidable Rohan has exercised his option to cancel the contract to make it null and void.

(iv) responsibilities of the beneficiary of the benefit under the void contract that is rendered void.

(v) Communication of recession

- A contract that is voidable at one party's discretion may be terminated, but such termination must be communicated to the other party in the same way as a proposal is.
- Recessions are subject to revocation in the same way that proposals are.

Effects of the promisee's disregard for the legitimate performance aids that the promisor has supplied.

Any promise who neglects to provide the promise with reasonable facilities for not keeping his promise is absolved of responsibility for any resulting failure to perform.: e.g.: If an apprentice refuses to learn, teacher cannot be held liable for not teaching

Discharge Of a contract

1. Discharge by performance

a. It occurs when the parties to the contract fulfil their contractual responsibilities in the manner specified.
b. Actual performance

Example: A sells his car to B for Rupees 1Cr, the car is delivered at the agreed place on the agreed time and B pays the agreed price and hence the contract ends by actual performance of the contract.

c. Discharge by mutual agreement:

The original contract does not have to be carried out if the parties agree to replace it with a new one, repudiate it, remit its obligations under it, or change it.

d. Discharge by impossibility of performance

It's possible that the impossibility was always there. That would make it impossible right away. Alternately, it could occur, Due to the possibility of supervening impossibility of:

i. An unforeseen change in laws
ii. The destruction of the subject - matter essential to that performance.
iii. the hon-existence or non -occurrence of particular state of things, which was naturally contemplated for performing the contract, as a result of some personal incapacity like dangerous malady
iv. The declaration of a war.

e. Discharge by lapse of time:

A party can be discharged from a contract if it is hat performed in reasonable time

f. Discharge by operation of law:
g. Discharge by breach of contract
h. Promise may wave or remit performance of promise
a. Effects of neglect of promise la afford promisor reasonable facilities for performance
j. Merger of rights.

CHAPTER SEVEN

BREACH OF CONTRACT AND IT'S REMEDIES

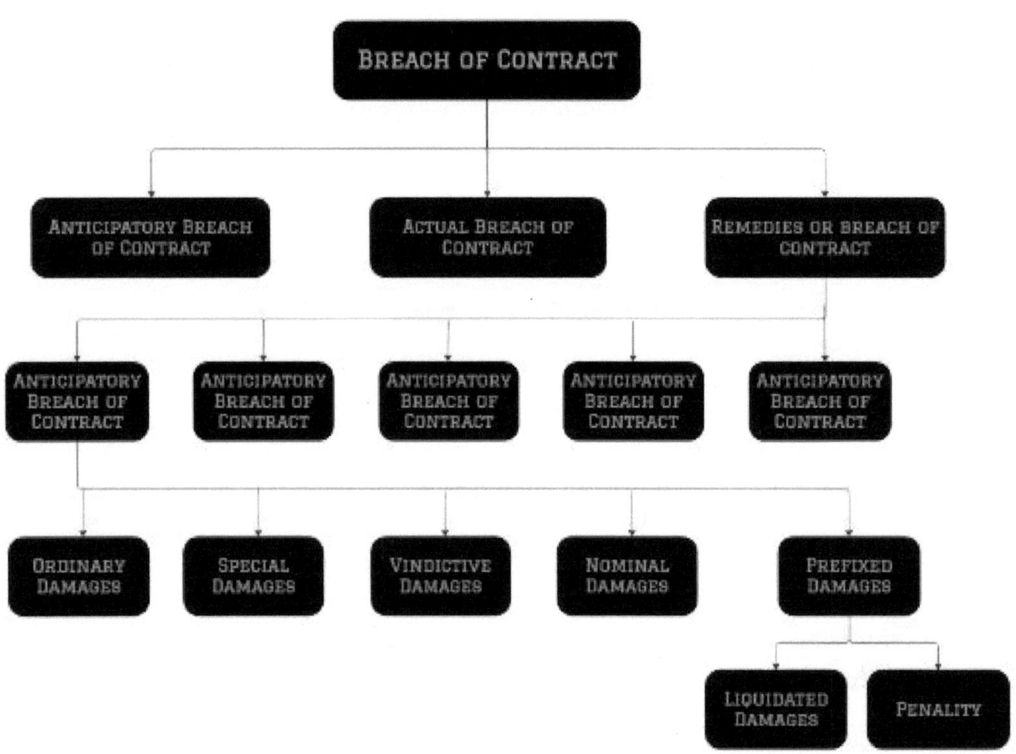

Actual Breach:

if a party fails to fulfil their obligation under the contract before the deadline. He or she is considered to have actually broken the law.

Anticipatory Breach:

On the other hand, anticipatory breach is considered to have occurred when a party terminates a contract before the time allotted for its execution has passed.

Anticipatory breach of Contract:

contract breach that is anticipated Anticipatory Breach is the legal term for a contract violation that occurs before the specified time for performance has passed and occurs when the promisor completely refuses to keep his word and makes his displeasure known before the time for performance has passed. Anticipatory breach of contract may take either of the following two ways

1. Expressly by words spoken or written and
2. Implied by the Conduct of one of the parties

Example 1) When A contracts with B to deliver 10 bales of cotton for a specific price on August 14 and B informs A on July 30 that he won't be able to deliver the cotton on August 14, the contract is expressly rejected.

Example 2) If "A" offers to sell "B" his white horse for Rs. 50,000 on August 10, 2016, but instead sells the horse to "C" on August 1, 2016, the promisor has engaged in anticipatory breach.

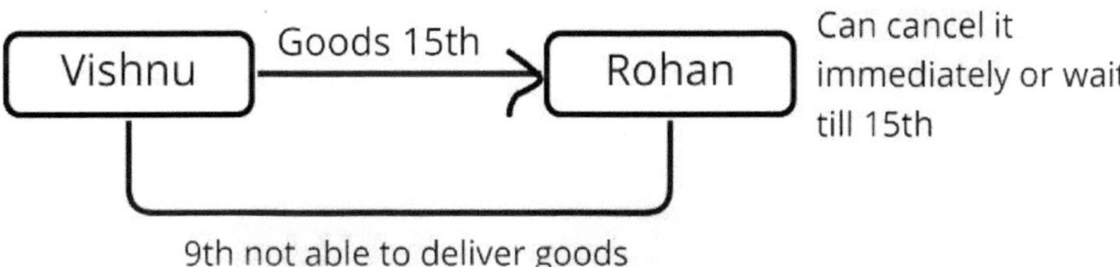

Effect of Anticipatory breach: -

Promise gets an option in case of anticipatory breach, and he can choose one.

1. Promisee Can cancel the contract immediately and can sue the other party for damages (or)
2. He can wait till the date of actual performance, or we might not Know it the promiser changes his mind and performs the contract -The guilty party can re consider and perform or can take the advantage of subsequent impossibility.

Example:

JKR entered into a contract with Javed Habib that he would dress his hair on 15/9 on 9/9, Javed Habib told JKR that he would not be able to honor the contract as he got another high-level commitment with Prabhas on 15 /9. Now JKR can immediately treat the contract cancelled and can sue Jared Habib for damage on 9/9 or JIR can wait till 19/9 as there is a possibility that Prabhas might cancel his commitment then maybe Javed Habib will honor JKR contract therefore he can wait till 15/9 as Javed Habib can still charge his mind and perform.

Actual breach of Contract:

Actual contract breach refers to the failure to fulfil as agreed upon on the appointed date.

The party that has been wronged gains the right to take legal action against the party who has broken his promise.

Actual breach of Contract may be committed

a. At the time when the performance of the contract is due

e.g.: Sneha was supposed to give Vasantha her Car an 15th though Vasantha was waiting for the car but Sneha did not give the car on 15th.

a. during the performance of the contract

e.g.: Sneha was supposed to teach Komal 5 units, but Sneha taught Komal only two units

Remedies Available

1. Suit for damages
2. - Recession of Contract

3. - Suit for specific performance
4. - Suit for injunction
5. - Suit upon quantum meruit.

Damages: -

The party who suffers due to a breach of contract has a right to compensation from the party who violated the agreement.

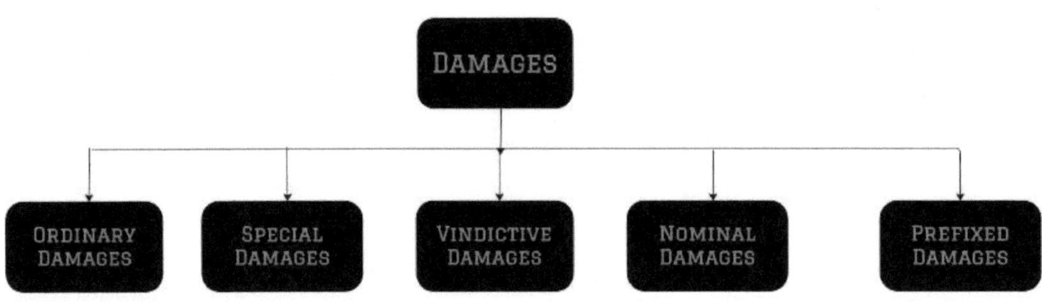

1. Ordinary damages:

Ordinary damages are those that are compensated for losses that resulted directly and naturally from the contract's breach.

Ordinary damages = Market price- contract price

Example: Anupama contracted to give her airplane to me on 20th of September far 1 crore on hire for 2 days on 16th of September Anupama informed that she wouldn't be able to perform the Contrack, Now I approached Bhumika for the airplane, Bhumika Charges 1 crore 10 thousand for hire per day for two days in this case I claim ordinary damages of 10,000 for Anupama.

2. Special damages:

Damages which arise due to some special a unusual circumstances can be recovered only if it is known to the parties at the time of entering into the contract can be claimed.

Example - A has made a contract with B. B should repair the machinery of A, B Is supposed to repair& give it back to A on 15th of October A was supposed to make some goods using that machinery and deliver it to C on 17th October. If A does that, he would receive a profit of Rs.10,00,000 B is aware this contract if B does not deliver the machinery by 15th A wouldn't be able to perform his contract to C.

So, A can claim Rs.10,00,000 Special damages from B as B was aware of the contract. It B had no Knowledge at the contract between A&C he wouldn't bel able to pay Rs. 10,00,000 as special damages.

3. Vindictive or exemplary damages these damages may be awarded in two cases:

- For wrongful dishonor by a banker of his customer's check because In this circumstance the injury due to wrongful dishonor to the drawer of cheque is so great that it causes loss of credit & reputation to him.
- For breach of contract to marry because it causes injury to his or her feelings.

4. Nominal damages:

Nominal damages are awarded where the plaintiff has proved that there has been a breach of contract, but he has not in fact suffered any real damage. It is awarded just to establish the right to decree for the breach of contract. The amount may be a rupee or even 10 paise.

5. Damages for deterioration caused by delay:

In this case of deterioration caused to good by delay, damages can be recovered from carrier even without notice. The word "deterioration" not only implies physical damages to the goods, but it may also mean. loss of special opportunity for sale.

6. Pre-fixed damages: -

Parties to a contract analyze at the time of its formation that on a breach of contract by any of them a certain amount will be payable as damage.

If a sum is named in a contract as the amount to be paid in case of a breach, the aggrieved party is entitled to receive from the party 'A' a reasonable compensation not exceeding the amount so named.

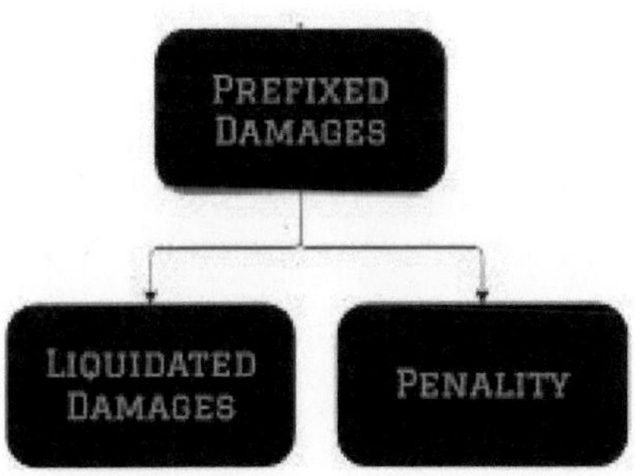

Enter Caption

i. Liquidated damages: -

Sometimes the parties to the contract pre-estimate the amount of damages which is reasonable & fair such amount is Known as liquidated damages.

Example: -

Shiva agreed to supply 100 apples to Hema Shree for Rs. 1000 and agreed that in case of breach defaulting party has to pay Rs. 200 as damage, here the parties have pre- estimated the amount of damages at the time of contract and the amount of damages at the time of contract and the amount of contract is reasonable hence it is called as liquidated damages.

ii. Penalty: -

The parties to the contract pre - estimate the amount of damage which is unreasonable and not fair such an amount is known as penalty.

Note: -

a. Unless both parties have genuinely experienced the identical loss, they are not entitled to compensation.
b. The date of the violation determines the amount of damages.
c. The main goal of awarding damages is to put the harmed party in the same situation that he would have been in if the contract violation hadn't happened.

In English law there is a distinction between penalty & liquidated damages.

But, in Indian law there is no difference between liquidated damages & penalty.

Exception to section 74:

When someone provides a bond to the federal or state government to carry out a public obligation or conduct that the public is interested in, if that person violates the terms of that bond, he will be required to pay the whole amount specified in that bond.

AL < PRD = PRD

AL> PRD = AL

Distinction between liquidated damages and penalty:

1. If the amount due is significantly greater than the portable harm for the violation, it is unquestionably a penalty.
2. When a payment is made in the event of default, the latter amount is a penalty because a simple payment delay is unlikely to result in harm.
3. The parties' expression is not conclusive. The court must determine if the amount specified in the contract is actually a fine or liquidated damages.
4. The violating party's payment of the agreed amount of money constitutes the essence of the penalty. A true pre-estimate of the loss constitutes the essence of liquidated damages.
5. Unlike English law, which distinguishes between liquidated damages and penalties, Indian law does not.

Besides claiming dame yes as a remedy for the breach of contract the following remedies are also available:

I. Recission of Contract:

The opposite party may treat a contract as cancelled when one party violates it. In this situation, he is released from all contractual duties and is entitled to compensation for any losses he may have incurred.

II. Quantum meruit: -

It means to pay remuneration for as much as work done or as much as benefited. The aggrieved party may file a suit for the payment remuneration in proportion to the work done by him.

Example: Aashrith agreed to paint Vishnu's 4 floored building, after finishing the work for two flours Vishnu did not allow Aashrith for the further work to be done Aashrith can claim compensation for the work, he has done on the two floors.

The clam for Quantum merit arises in the following Cases:

a. Whenever a contract is found to be invalid or when it expires.
b. when something is carried out without any thought of gratuity.
c. When there is an express or inferred agreement to provide services but no compensation is specified
d. when a contract is divisible and the party not in default has taken use of the benefit at par performance
e. when one party abandons or refuses to perform the contract. When an indivisibles contract calls for a lump sum.
f. When a contract is fully completed but poorly executed, the party who carried out the job may claim the lump money, but the other party may deduct for the poor performance.

III. Suit for specific performance:

In cases of contract breach where damages are insufficient, the court may, at its discretion, order the party in breach to fulfil his commitment in accordance with the provisions of the contract by ordering particular performance.

Example: we signed Virat Kohli for a movie, and we also signed Anushka Sharma in the lead role. Virat Kohli breaches the contract the remedy available to us Is we can go to the court and demand Virat Kohli to be the actor as promise in the contract. So here we are demanding Virat's special performance. As no amount of Money can replace the damage cart to Us.

IV. Suit for injunction: -

When one of the parties to a contract is violating its terms, the court may issue a "injunction order" prohibiting that party from breaking his commitment.

Example: Prabhas agreed to Act exclusively for Rajamouli for one year. During the year he contracted to act for Vasantha. Here he could be restrained by injunction.

References

1. *ARRANGEMENT OF SECTIONS ____________ SECTIONS PREAMBLE.* (n.d.). https://legislative.gov.in/sites/default/files/A1872-09.pdf
2. chettoor, S. (1970, January 1). *Ignorance of law: Can it be an excuse?* Www.indiainfoline.com. https://www.indiainfoline.com/article/news-sector-others/ignorance-of-law-can-it-be-an-excuse-113111404453_1.html#:~:text=Lord%20Ellenborough%20said%20%E2%80%9Cthere%20is
3. garg, A. kumar. (2020, July 19). *Evolution of law in India.* Lawcian. https://www.lawcian.com/post/evolution-of-law-in-india
4. *JURISPRUDENCE, INTERPRETATION AND GENERAL LAWS.* (n.d.). THE INSTITUTE of COMPANY SECRETARIES of INDIA. https://www.icsi.edu/media/webmodules/JI_&_GL_FINAL_01112021.pdf
5. *Legal evolution.* (2021, April 23). Wikipedia. https://en.wikipedia.org/wiki/Legal_evolution
6. Younkins, E. W. (2000, August 5). *THE EVOLUTION OF LAW.* Www.quebecoislibre.org. http://www.quebecoislibre.org/000805-11.htm#:~:text=The%20evolution%20of%20law%20began

Printed by Libri Plureos GmbH in Hamburg,
Germany